FREE TO THRIVE

A Curriculum Empowering You to Live Your Best Life

By Harmony Dust, MSW

Live Free Volume 1
Free to Thrive: A Curriculum Empowering You to Live Your Best Life

Copyright 2023 by Harmony Dust

All Rights Reserved. No part of Live Free Volume 1, Free to Thrive: A Curriculum Empowering You to Live Your Best Life may not be reproduced, stored in a retrieval system, or transmitted, in any form or by any means—by electronic, mechanical, photocopying, recording or otherwise—in any form without permission. Thank you for buying an authorized edition of this book and for complying with copyright laws.

Harmony Dust
PO Box 5311
Sherman Oaks, CA 91413
info@iamatreasure.com
www.iamatreasure.com

Unless otherwise noted, all Scripture quotations are from The Passion Translation®. Copyright © 2017, 2018, 2020 by Passion & Fire Ministries, Inc. Used by permission. All rights reserved. ThePassionTranslation.com.Used by permission.

Cover Design by Moonwalker Digital
Interior Design by Moonwalker Digital
Illustration by Moonwalker Digital

Published by Treasures Ministries 501 (c) (3)

Paperback ISBN: 978-0-9863338-6-6

First Edition

Ordering Information:
Special discounts are available for large quantity purchases. Please contact the publisher by email: info@iamatreasure.com or visit www.iamatreasure.com for more details.

Printed in the United States.

This material is protected by copyright law, and reproduction, including photocopying, is strictly prohibited.

This workbook is dedicated to Denise Roman and Monique Calderon. Your pursuit of freedom and dedication to empowering others is breathtaking.

Special thanks to Melissa Thomas, Lindsay Hall, and Monique Calderon for editing and consulting.

This workbook belongs to:

_____

Safety Check

If you are in an unsafe situation, we encourage you to get additional help.

Domestic Violence Hotline: 800-799-7233
National Trafficking Hotline: 888-373-7888

If you are in immediate danger, please call 911.

Table of Contents

10	WELCOME LETTER	79	WHAT IS LOVE?
12	THE INVITATION	90	BOUNDARIES
18	RESILIENT	111	CORE VALUES
23	YOU'VE GOT WHAT IT TAKES	118	THE LIFE YOU WANT
27	WHO'S GOT YOUR BACK?	128	FREE TO DREAM
34	GRATITUDE	141	IT'S A MIRACLE
40	A MENTAL GLOW-UP	146	WISDOM TO KNOW THE DIFFERENCE
55	WHAT GIVES YOU LIFE?	154	FREE TO CHANGE
60	WHAT KEEPS YOU GROUNDED?	169	A LEAP OF FAITH
67	DEALING WITH DIFFICULTIES	180	YOU DID IT!

"My *mission in life* is not merely to survive, but to thrive; and to do so with some passion, some compassion, some humor, and some style."

Maya Angelou

Dear Treasure,

I am so glad you are here!

Let me start by telling you this- I do not love everything I have gone through, but I love the person I've become in the process.

I have experienced the trauma of abuse in many of its forms. I am all too familiar with devastating grief and loss. I know the deep pain of betrayal and the heartbreak of abandonment. I know what it is like to become stuck in toxic relationships. I know what it feels like to be exploited-my body turned into a product and sold in strip clubs. Each night, I handed all of my money over to a man- no, a pimp- who preyed on my vulnerability and pretended to love me.

I know the cost of staying. And I know the strength and determination it takes to leave.

I have fought for my healing and freedom. In the process, I discovered that recovery is not easy, but it is worth it. And I am worth it.

Today, I am living out so many of my dreams. Including and especially my dream of encouraging other women on their journey to live healthy, thriving lives. In 2003, I founded Treasures, an organization that provides outreach and support to women in the sex industry and survivors of trafficking. Through the work of Treasures, my pain has been turned into purpose. I still go through hard things, just like everyone else... but there is far more joy than pain, far more peace than chaos, and far more love than heartbreak.

As the opening quote from Maya Angelou says,

> "My mission in life is not merely to survive, but to thrive; and to do so with some passion, some compassion, some humor, and some style."

I believe we are designed to thrive. I believe it is never too late for a new beginning and that the dreams of our heart, no matter how broken, dormant, or dead, can still be brought to life.

I want you to know that you are not alone. There are hundreds and thousands of women, just like you and me, who have overcome insurmountable odds and dared to believe in the beauty of their dreams.

My hope is that this workbook will inspire you to clarify your desires, strengths and values, equip you with empowering skills, and encourage you to move toward the future you dream of. My hope is that you will thrive!

Love,

Harmony

The Invitation

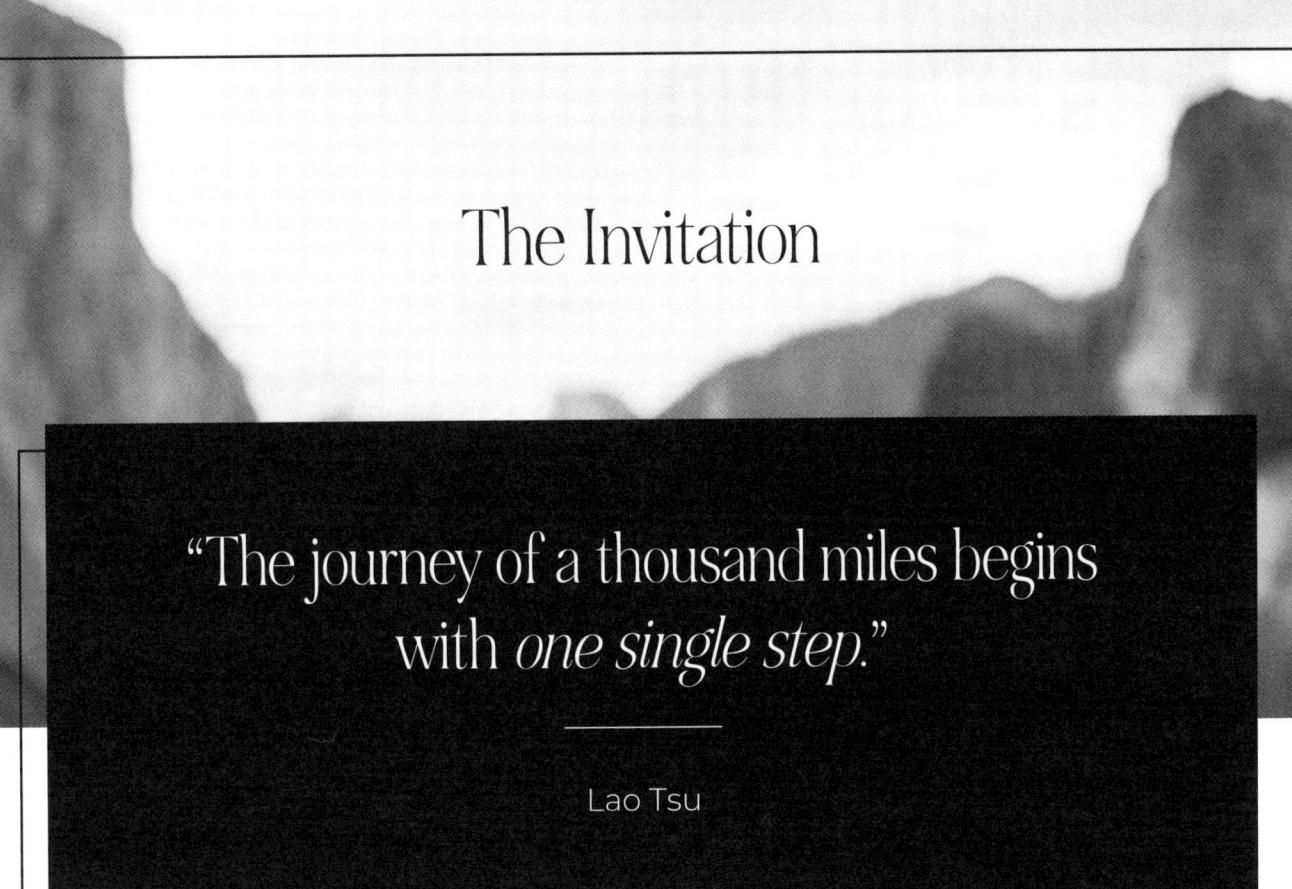

"The journey of a thousand miles begins with *one single step.*"

Lao Tsu

This is *your* life. You are the only one who can live it.

This workbook is meant to empower you to move toward your best life. It is an invitation to explore your dreams, desires, wants, and needs in order to discover your best next steps. <u>You</u> get to decide what your journey will look like, every step of the way. That is not to say that there will not be barriers, obstacles and challenges along the way, but I believe that you, brave one, have what it takes to overcome them and to live a thriving, flourishing life.

Take a deep breath. Like, for real. I encourage you to stop right now and take a big, beautiful spacious breath.

And another one.

And one more.

Do you feel that? The air coursing through your lungs is telling you something.

You are still here.

You have made it this far. Maybe there were times when you thought you wouldn't. But you are still living and breathing, and as long as there is breath in your lungs, there is always, always hope.

You don't have to have it all figured out. You just have to be willing to take the next best step for you. Right now, maybe that next step is as simple as continuing to the next page of this workbook.

ARE YOU WILLING?

☐ Yes

☐ No

☐ I'm not sure, but I will turn the page anyway

Check Your Feelings

———

One of the ways I survived in my old life was to disconnect from my feelings. I spent so much time trying to push away the pain, run from feelings I was afraid of and pretend I was okay, that I lost touch with my feelings. Even the happy ones. I was numb.

Research shows that checking in with our feelings and naming them can help us feel more calm. It also helps build mindfulness and self-awareness. Throughout this workbook, from time to time, we will invite you to name your own feelings. If you are new to the practice of identifying your feelings, this might feel challenging at first. But you've got this!

TOO MUCH TOO SOON?

If naming your feelings is too much too soon, you can circle one of the thumbs below that best describes your mood and move onto the next section.

Ready to name your feelings?

Using the chart below, circle which feeling(s) you are having...

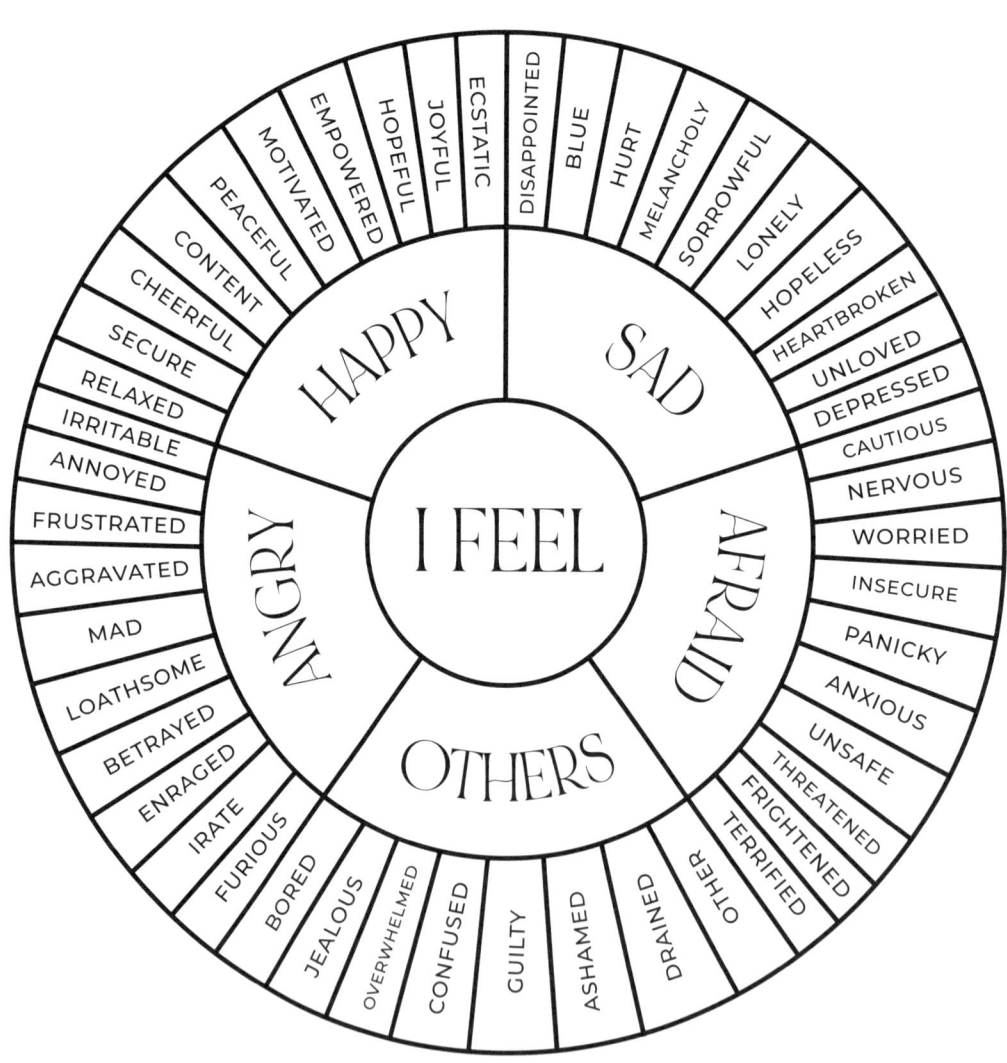

FUN FACT

I have a chart like this on my refrigerator. I bought it to help teach my children to regularly check in with their feelings, but I use it too!

What do you need?

Feelings are signals. They invite us to pay attention to what is happening around us and help dictate how we respond. Often, underneath our emotions are needs waiting to be met. The diagram below shows examples of this.

IF FEELINGS COULD TALK

 **SADNESS** might be telling me i need **TO CRY**	**LONELINESS** might be telling me i need **CONNECTION**	**SHAME** might be telling me i need **SELF-COMPASSION**	**RESENTMENT** might be telling me i need **TO FORGIVE**
EMPTINESS might be telling me i need **TO DO SOMETHING CREATIVE**	**ANGER** might be telling me i need **TO CHECK-IN WITH MY BOUNDARIES**	 **ANXIETY** might be telling me i need **TO BREATHE**	**STRESS** might be telling me i need **TO TAKE IT ONE STEP AT A TIME**

Illustration based on 'If Feelings Could Talk: A Free Social Emotional Learning Poster' by wholeheartedschoolcounseling.com

Based on how you are feeling right now, what do you need?

If you are feeling great, take a moment to celebrate this. If you are experiencing any difficult emotions, you might call someone on your support team or do something calming/uplifting like going for a walk. Refer to the diagram above for additional examples.

I FEEL

I NEED

Resilient

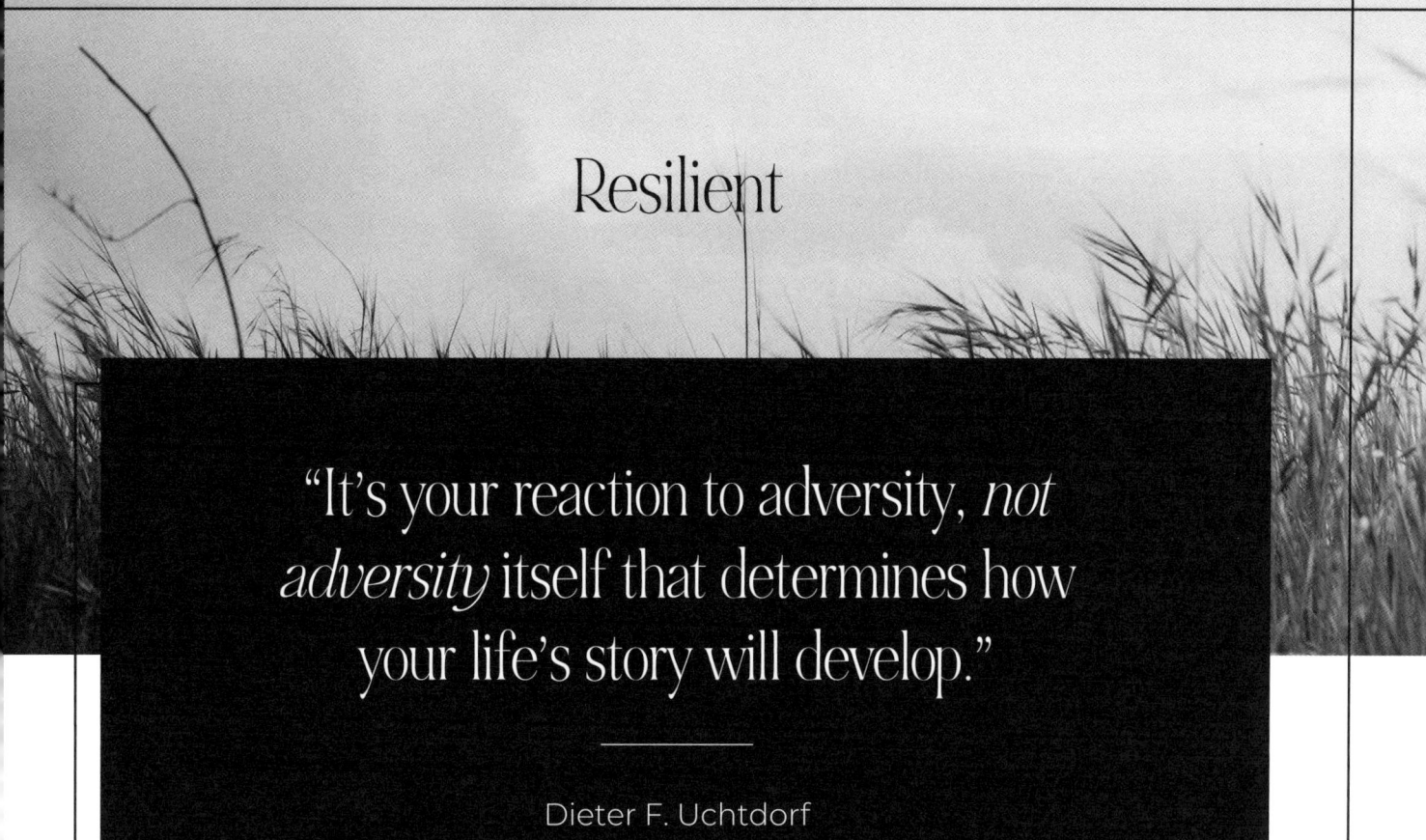

> "It's your reaction to adversity, *not adversity* itself that determines how your life's story will develop."
>
> Dieter F. Uchtdorf

Pain. Uncertainty. Injustice. Loss. These are just a few of the inescapable realities of life. Some find themselves faced with more adversity than others. When circumstances are beyond my control, which they often are, I find strength and comfort in the fact that there is always one thing within my control... how I respond to adversity.

I am constantly in awe of the resilience of the human spirit. Our capacity to recover from the pain and difficulties life seems to dish out so plentifully is truly astounding. Many of the women who inspire me the most have been through unthinkable trauma, yet, they remain standing with miraculously tender hearts, a fierce determination to encourage others and a desire to leave the world a better place. To sum it up, they are resilient.

Resilient [ri-**zil**-yuhnt, -**zil**-ee-uhnt][2]

1. springing back; rebounding.
2. returning to the original form or position after being bent, compressed, or stretched.
3. recovering readily from illness, depression, adversity, or the like; buoyant.

Our ability to rebound and recover is truly astonishing. And it begs the question, what makes us resilient?

Pediatrician and human development expert, Kenneth Ginsburg, M.D. suggests that there are 7 building blocks that make up resilience, known as the 7 C's of resilience.

As we increase our capacity to overcome and recover from difficulties, we will be free to thrive and live to our fullest potential.

[2] *Dictionary.com*

The 7 C's of Resilience

01 COMPETENCE
the ability to handle situations effectively

02 CONFIDENCE
the belief in one's abilities or capabilities

03 CONNECTION
a sense of closeness with/attachment to people and community

04 CHARACTER
a fundamental sense of right and wrong that enables us to stick to our values

05 CONTRIBUTION
a sense that we can make the world a better place through our contributions

06 COPING
our capacity to manage and respond to stress

07 CONTROL
the belief that we have the ability to make choices that will impact outcomes in our lives

Resilience is key to a thriving life.

If we are going to truly thrive, we are going to have to bounce back from some things. Since strengthening our resilience is a vital part of being empowered to flourish, each section in this workbook is designed to help you cultivate at least one building block of resilience.

My guess is, you have already developed quite a bit of resilience in your years here on this planet. You may find that you are especially skilled in a few of the 7 C's of resilience listed above. You may also discover that there are other areas where you recognize opportunities for growth. My hope is that this workbook will support you in sharpening the skills you already have and strengthening the skills you are still developing.

REFLECT

As you consider the 7 C's of resilience, in what ways have you witnessed resilience in yourself? In other words, which of the 7 C's have you relied on to recover from difficulties?

Which of the 7 C's of resilience would you most like to cultivate?

You've Got What it Takes!

DISCOVERING YOUR STRENGTHS

RESILIENCE BUILDING BLOCKS: CONFIDENCE AND COMPETENCE

> "Know that *there is something inside you* that is greater than any obstacle."
>
> — Christian D. Larson

You may not be exactly where you want to be, but you are still here! And that is not an accident. If you are reading this right now, I am assuming you have already faced insurmountable odds. You have gone through things that could have taken you out… but they didn't!

You are one of a kind. No one else in all creation–in all of history– can live the life you were created to live. You have a unique set of gifts, strengths and abilities that have gotten you this far and will help propel you to where you desire to go. I truly believe that the strengths inside of you are far greater than any obstacle you can encounter.

To live our best lives, we can continue to develop and draw from what is already in us. Of course, we all have weaknesses and areas where we can grow and improve, but studies show that when we focus on our strengths (also known as taking a strength-based approach) we feel more confident, self-aware and productive.[3]

So, take a moment to identify some of the strengths you already have.

[3] *https://www.gallup.com/learning/248405/strengths-development-coaching.aspx*

Review the list below and circle all of the strengths you can see in yourself. If you need some help, ask someone who cares about you what strengths they see in you.

Strength/streNG(k)TH/: [4]
a positive or valuable attribute or quality

ADAPTABLE	FLEXIBLE	PATIENT
ADVENTUROUS	FOCUSED	PEACEFUL
AMBITIOUS	FRIENDLY	PERSISTENT
ANALYTICAL	FUNNY	PERSUASIVE
ARTISTIC	GENEROUS	RESOURCEFUL
ATHLETIC	GRATEFUL	RESPONSIBLE
CARING	HONEST	SPIRITUAL
COMMITTED	HUMBLE	STRAIGHTFORWARD
COMMUNICATOR	INCLUSIVE	STRATEGIC
COMPASSIONATE	INTELLIGENT	THOUGHTFUL
CONSISTENT	KIND	THRIFTY
COURAGEOUS	LEARNER	TIMELY
CREATIVE	LOGICAL	TRUSTWORTHY
DETAIL-ORIENTED	MOTIVATED	VISIONARY
DETERMINED	OPTIMISTIC	WISE
DISCIPLINED	ORGANIZED	OTHER: _____
EMPATHETIC	OUTGOING	

[4] *https://www.dictionary.com/browse/strength*

REFLECT

Of the strengths you circled,
which ones do you believe are your top 5?

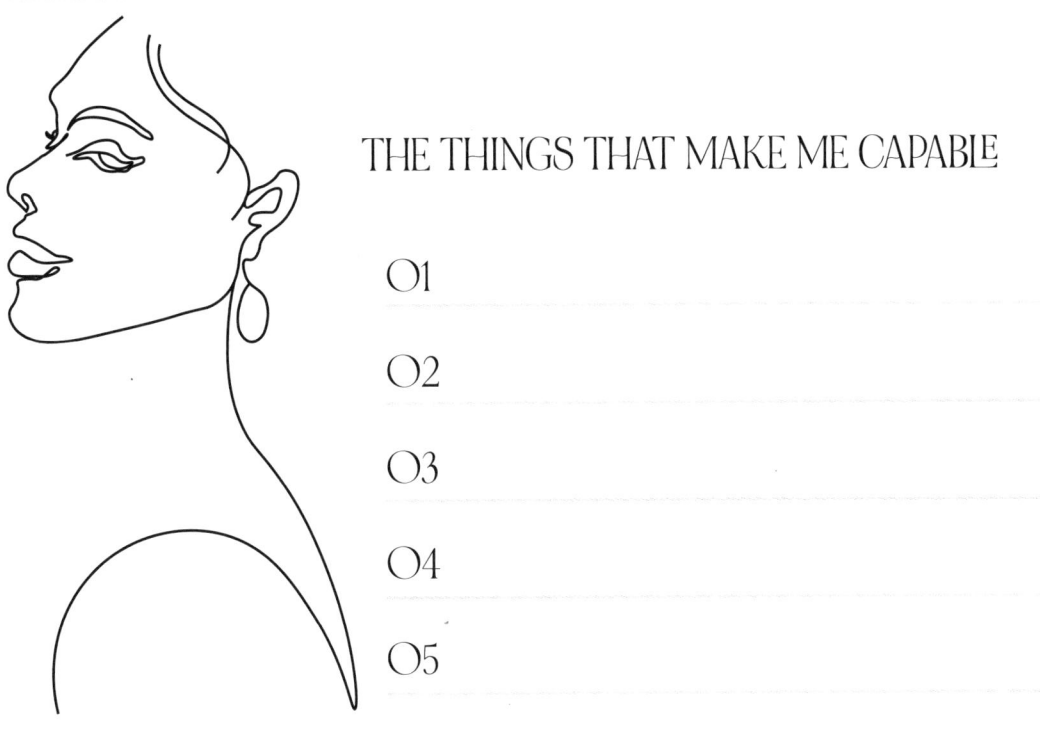

THE THINGS THAT MAKE ME CAPABLE

O1

O2

O3

O4

O5

In what ways do you believe your strengths can help
you as you move forward on your journey?

Who's Got Your Back?

IDENTIFY YOUR SUPPORT SYSTEM

RESILIENCE BUILDING BLOCK: CONNECTION

> Lying, thinking
> Last night
> How to find my soul a home
> Where water is not thirsty
> And bread loaf is not stone
> *I came up with one thing*
> And I don't believe I'm wrong
> That nobody,
> But nobody
> Can make it out here alone.
>
> ―― Maya Angelou

In all my years of supporting others as they rebuild their lives and pursue their dreams, I have noticed that those of us who have managed to truly thrive have had one thing in common: we didn't do it alone. Whether it was a trusted friend, family member, therapist, support group, mentor, or a combination of all of these, we had someone in our corner, encouraging us along the way.

I recognize that relationships themselves can be the source of so much pain. If you, like me, have experienced betrayal, abuse, and exploitation (or any one of these things) choosing to trust people again can be challenging. We may even try to convince ourselves that isolation is the only way to protect ourselves from getting hurt again.

I know the pain of relational trauma. I also know the healing and freedom I have experienced through healthy, restorative relationships. I believe the risk of inviting people into your process is worth it.

As you lean into becoming all that you are created to be and pursue your best life, I encourage you to find *at least* one safe, caring person who can be a consistent ally for you. Seeking support from empathetic individuals who prioritize your safety, well-being, and agency can help rebuild your trust in humanity.

Experiencing safe and nurturing relationships can lay the foundation for restoring your ability to trust and form healthy connections.

I acknowledge this might feel unattainable for some. There was a time it felt pretty impossible for me as well. A mountain of pain, fear of being hurt or rejected and an arsenal of defense mechanisms designed to keep me safe, created a lot of barriers to building healthy relationships. It took time to work through all of that. We will address how to navigate these barriers to fulfilling relationships in future volumes of this workbook series, but for now, be encouraged that the more you tend to your heart and pursue healing and wholeness, the more tangible healthy relationships will become.

You deserve to have a support network that nourishes your well-being and supports your growth.

Look for safe people who...

- Respect you
- Bring out the best in you
- Will cheer you on as you grow
- Will value who you are

Growing My Support System

On the next page, you'll be invited to write the names of anyone who is currently in your support system.

I recognize that this particular activity may be challenging. When I first left my exploiter and the people I was connected to in "the life", I felt incredibly lonely and isolated. It took time to build new connections. If you are building a support system from scratch or have had difficulty forming new relationships, don't give up.

Please know that Treasures is here for you. We have virtual support groups specifically designed to build a sense of community among women who have worked in the sex industry and/or experienced trafficking. You can call or email us for more info. And we would be honored to be written on one of your petals in the exercise below.

TREASURES: 818-963-1477 | care@iamatreasure.com

MY SUPPORT SYSTEM

Write the names of anyone who is currently in your support system on the petals of the flower below. Then, write the name of one or more safe people you would like to invite to be a part of your support system. **Feel free to get creative and add some color to your flower.**

Reach Out

Once you have thought about the people you would like to invite to be a part of your support system, the next step is to reach out to them. This might feel scary or awkward, but bravely doing so can be a game-changer. People won't know what you want and need unless you tell them. You might say something as simple as this…

> *I plan to spend some time clarifying my goals and dreams and I could use some extra encouragement. I also want to intentionally invest in healthy relationships and build a stronger support system.*
>
> *Would you be open to me reaching out to you from time to time?*
> *Or*
> *Would you be open to getting coffee and meeting up from time to time?*

WHEN YOU NEED EXTRA SUPPORT...

It is wonderful to have friends in your corner. But there might be times when you need more support than they are able to give. When I am going through a crisis or processing some really hard things, I understand that as much as my friends love me, they aren't therapists and there are certain things they can't do or give. They might not be able to come through for me in all of the ways that I need. This is when I seek to add professional healing resources to my support network.

Other steps I can take to build a support system
(Check all of the ideas you may wish to try).

- [ ] Identify someone I want to get to know better and reach out
- [ ] Ask someone who has already built a support system what program they have found helpful
- [ ] Email care@iamatreasure.com for info on mentors, support groups and additional referrals to resources
- [ ] Visit https://humantraffickinghotline.org to find resources in your area
- [ ] Visit www.celebraterecovery.org or google "12-Step meetings near me" for 12-step programs
- [ ] Go to a service in a faith community
- [ ] Other _____

Gratitude

RESILIENCE BUILDING BLOCK: COPING

"A *grateful heart* is a magnet for miracles."

Unknown

Gratitude is about noticing and appreciating the goodness in our lives. It does not mean we deny the reality of what is hard, challenging, or unjust, but it does mean we make it a practice to tune into those things that are good and beautiful and lovely— the things that spark joy and cultivate hope.

I acknowledge that gratitude comes easier to some than others and that it is easier to practice in some seasons than in others. There have been many days when I have had to struggle through heartache and grief to find something worthy of gratitude. When all else fails and the whole world seems like it is crashing down around me, I remember the way the sun glistens on the ocean like dancing diamonds, or the little clouds of softness that are my children's cheeks—and for these things, I can find it in my heart to be grateful.

I do believe that intentionally cultivating a heart of gratitude can be a powerful and magnetic thing. Personal opinions and experiences aside, however, research supports this idea as well. Numerous studies have shown that gratitude improves our health, happiness, and overall well-being. For these reasons, I believe practicing gratitude is a key component of a thriving life.

A simple way to practice gratitude....

1. Notice the goodness and beauty around you. Search for it. If it feels difficult for you to find beauty right now, perhaps you can connect to the beauty of your own breath. Can you connect to the fact that every minute you are alive, your body continues to nourish itself by taking in life-giving oxygen and eliminating the carbon dioxide our body no longer needs?

2. Absorb and savor the goodness you discover.

3. Express your gratitude. Write it down. Say it outloud. Whisper it in a prayer. Share your gratitude with others.

4. Set a daily alarm as a reminder to stop and notice the good around you.

REFLECT

What feelings does the practice of gratitude bring up for you?

What has your experience with gratitude been?
Does gratitude come easily to you? Does it feel challenging?

PRACTICE

Name what you are grateful for...
It can be a sound, a place, a person or anything
in all creation that sparks joy or relief for you.

THINGS I AM GRATEFUL FOR...

○ 1

○ 2

○ 3

○ 4

MAKING GRATITUDE A PRACTICE...

In my experience, gratitude is sort of a muscle. The more you use it, the more it grows and the more powerful it becomes. Making a habit or practice of gratitude requires intention and practice. Here are some simple ways to do this....

- ☐ Keep a gratitude journal and write in it daily
- ☐ Keep a gratitude jar on your coffee table and fill it with notes you jot down about things you are grateful for
- ☐ Spend a few minutes each day reflecting, meditating, or praying about what you are grateful for

Do you believe cultivating a practice of gratitude would be beneficial to you? If so, how?

Are you experiencing any resistance towards gratitude? If so, where do you think this might be coming from? Is this something you might want to process with one of the safe people you identified earlier?

Do you have a plan for how you might like to practice gratitude more regularly? If so, please describe.

A Mental Glow-Up

RESILIENCE BUILDING BLOCKS: CONFIDENCE AND COPING

> "Watch your thoughts, they become your words; watch your words, they become your actions; *watch your actions, they become your habits*; watch your habits, they become your character; watch your character, it becomes your destiny."
>
> — Lao Tzu

As I write this, the hashtag #glowup has over 87 BILLION views on Tik Tok.

87 BILLION!

Most of them are about one thing: physical appearance. The posts are primarily documenting glow-ups involving weight loss and fitness (with and without surgery), sprinkled with some hair, skin, and makeup glow-ups.

Even for those of use who are not obsessed with the glow-up phenomenon, some of us spend significant time each day tending to our outer appearance. Just to get ready in the morning, we use an entire arsenal of equipment—hair products, dryers, irons, lotions and sprays, body scrubs, skin care products and make-up. This isn't a bad thing. It is good to take care of our physical selves. This is a part of self-care.

After leaving the sex industry, I actually went through a period where I pretty much ditched all of those practices. It felt good for my livelihood not to depend on my looks and I basically wanted to hide from any and all attention. To keep it real, nowadays, in these work-from-home post-pandemic days, I am lucky if I get a brush through my hair!

Still, there have been many days when I have spent significantly more time focused on my physical self than my inner self. I can't show up to work looking like I just rolled out of bed. So, when I am short on time, it is easier to neglect my mind than my body.

The truth is, a thriving life requires that we are as diligent about caring for our inner-selves as we are our outer-selves. Our thought patterns and self-talk play a critical role in influencing our feelings, decisions, and actions.

A mental glow-up isn't an easy process by any means, but it is absolutely good. Here are three key practices that will guide you to a healthier version of yourself…

1. Think About What You Are Thinking About

In order to identify the untrue, negative and unhelpful thoughts that might be shaping our lives, we need to think about what we are thinking about. Identifying our negative thoughts is the first step in changing them.

You may even want to commit to spending the next week intentionally focusing on how you talk to yourself and noticing the tone of your thoughts.

Here are some questions to consider when evaluating your thoughts…

- Is it kind and compassionate?
- Is it critical or cruel?
- Is it blaming or shaming?
- Does this thought inspire me to live my best life or be my best self?

2. Don't Believe The Lies

I used to believe a lot of lies. They were so woven into the fabric of my being that they became my personal truth. I believed that I was worthless, stupid, and unlovable. Some of these lies were spoken to me or about me, and I adopted them as my own. Others were formed out of experiences of abuse, abandonment, and rejection.

My life reflected what I thought to be true because I made choices based on those deep beliefs. In essence, my thoughts shaped my beliefs, and my beliefs determined my actions and habits. Ultimately, what I thought to be true about myself kept me stuck in toxic relationships.

Even today, those old lies pop up from time to time, but they are quieter and easier to combat with more positive and truthful thoughts. This didn't happen overnight. It took time and consistent effort on my part to retrain my brain.

Transformation requires action. In order to live our most thriving life, many of us will need to proactively identify and replace the lies we have come to believe. Doing so will take some intentional effort. I will provide you with examples of truths and an opportunity to practice replacing the lies at the end of this section.

3. Ask Yourself, "What Would You Say To Your Friend?"

Chances are, if your friend came to you for encouragement, you would not tell them many of the negative things you think to yourself. Often, it is easier to be kind to others than it is to be kind to ourselves.

As I work to make-over my mind, I have found it helpful to challenge myself...*If I wouldn't talk to a friend that way, why is it okay for me to talk to myself that way?*

As you consider your own thought patterns, ask yourself, "What would I say to my friend?"

REFLECT

As you reflect on your self-talk/thought patterns, what words and phrases come to your mind? Is there something you repeatedly think or tell yourself? List those things here.

Are any of the thoughts from the list you made above negative, untrue and/or unhelpful?

Can you identify where the untrue, negative, and unhelpful thoughts may be coming from? For example, were they initiated by someone else's words? Or did they originate with a specific experience such as abuse, abandonment, or rejection? If it feels safe for you to explore this, please describe. If it feels like too much to explore on your own right now, I encourage you to honor that feeling and move on to the next question.

How do you suspect your thoughts might be shaping your life?

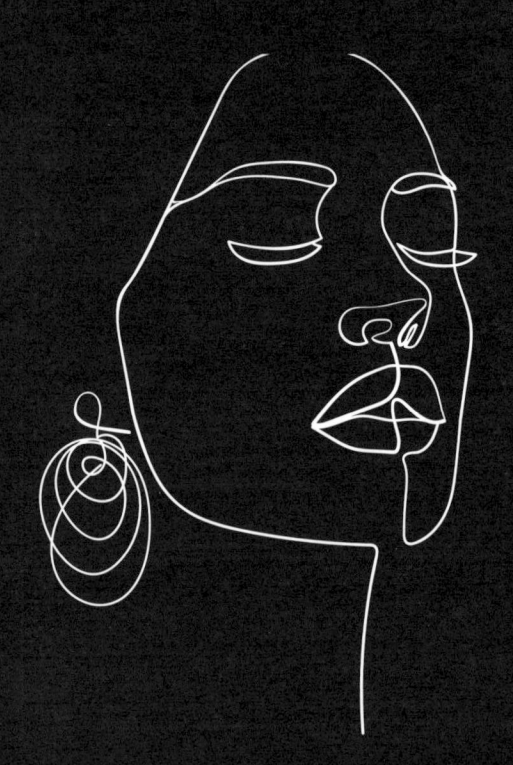

In the space below, write down the negative, untrue or unhelpful thoughts that take up residence in your mind. Then, write the true, helpful or positive thoughts you can focus on replacing them with. I have included some examples for you to draw from. And remember, ask yourself, "What would I say to my friend?"

If you need some help with this exercise, consider reaching out to a trusted friend, therapist or mentor.

UNTRUE, UNHELPFUL OR NEGATIVE BELIEF	TRUE, HELPFUL OR POSITIVE BELIEF
I am unloveable.	I am loved and lovable. Love is always flowing to me and through me.
My life is pointless.	I have been created with a purpose, and there is hope for my future.
I am a failure.	Mistakes are a part of life. I am allowed to make them. I can learn and grow from them.
It's too late for me.	It is never too late for another chance. Each day is a new beginning for me.

UNTRUE, UNHELPFUL OR NEGATIVE BELIEF	TRUE, HELPFUL OR POSITIVE BELIEF
I will never be able to XYZ.	I am capable of doing whatever I set my mind to.
I need to lose weight or change XYZ about my body.	I love my body as it is today. My body is
I am worthless.	I am valuable. My value cannot be diminished.
I am not good enough.	I am enough—right now, today, just as I am.
I always seem to fall short.	I don't have to be perfect to be perfectly loved.
It's selfish of me to take care of myself.	Caring for myself is not selfish. It's necessary.
I don't have time to focus on my growth and healing.	I don't have time _not_ to focus on my growth and healing.

MENTAL GLOW-UP

In the spaces below, write the true, helpful, and positive beliefs you would like to create more space for in your mind.

HOW MIGHT YOUR LIFE LOOK DIFFERENT IF THESE WERE THE THOUGHTS THAT OCCUPIED YOUR MIND?

Pro Tip: Write down some of the truths you want to focus on and put them in places where you will see them often; your bathroom mirror, the fridge, in your car, at your desk, etc.

ARE YOU READY FOR A MENTAL GLOW-UP?

Changing our thinking is a process that requires intention and effort. Every time you find yourself playing those old mental recordings, are you willing to commit to redirecting your thinking to the truth?

☐ Yes, I commit!

_____
SIGN HERE

Check Your Feelings

Now that you have completed
a few more sections, it's time for another
feelings check-in...

TOO MUCH TOO SOON?

If naming your feelings is too much too soon, you can circle one of the thumbs below that best describes your mood and move onto the next section.

👍 🤚 👎

Ready to name your feelings?

Using the chart below, circle which feeling(s) you are having...

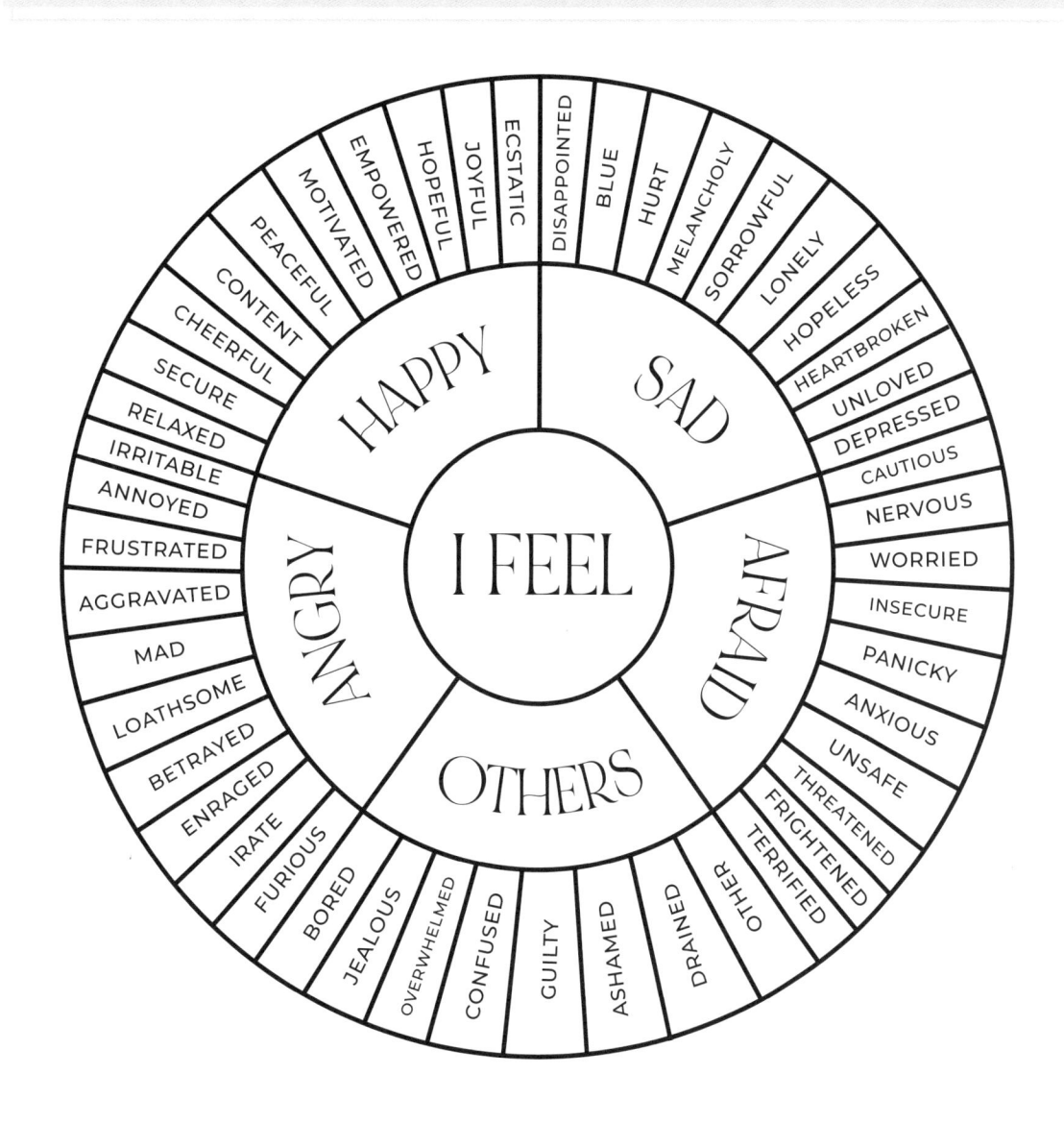

I FEEL

HAPPY: ECSTATIC, JOYFUL, HOPEFUL, EMPOWERED, MOTIVATED, PEACEFUL, CONTENT, CHEERFUL

SAD: DISAPPOINTED, BLUE, HURT, MELANCHOLY, SORROWFUL, LONELY, HOPELESS, HEARTBROKEN, UNLOVED, DEPRESSED

AFRAID: CAUTIOUS, NERVOUS, WORRIED, INSECURE, PANICKY, ANXIOUS, UNSAFE, THREATENED, FRIGHTENED, TERRIFIED

ANGRY: SECURE, RELAXED, IRRITABLE, ANNOYED, FRUSTRATED, AGGRAVATED, MAD, LOATHSOME, BETRAYED, ENRAGED, IRATE, FURIOUS

OTHERS: BORED, JEALOUS, OVERWHELMED, CONFUSED, GUILTY, ASHAMED, DRAINED, OTHER

What do you need?

Feelings are signals. They invite us to pay attention to what is happening around us and help dictate how we respond. Often, underneath our emotions are needs waiting to be met. The diagram below shows examples of this.

IF FEELINGS COULD TALK

SADNESS might be telling me i need **TO CRY**	**LONELINESS** might be telling me i need **CONNECTION**	**SHAME** might be telling me i need **SELF-COMPASSION**	**RESENTMENT** might be telling me i need **TO FORGIVE**
EMPTINESS might be telling me i need **TO DO SOMETHING CREATIVE**	**ANGER** might be telling me i need **TO CHECK-IN WITH MY BOUNDARIES**	**ANXIETY** might be telling me i need **TO BREATHE**	**STRESS** might be telling me i need **TO TAKE IT ONE STEP AT A TIME**

Illustration based on 'If Feelings Could Talk: A Free Social Emotional Learning Poster' by wholeheartedschoolcounseling.com

Based on how you are feeling right now, what do you need?

If you are feeling great, take a moment to celebrate this. If you are experiencing any difficult emotions, you might call someone on your support team or do something calming/uplifting like going for a walk. Refer to the diagram above for additional examples.

I FEEL

I NEED

What Gives You Life?

RESILIENCE BUILDING BLOCK: COPING

> "Self-Care is *not self-indulgence*, it is self-preservation..."
>
> Audre Lorde

Being human can be hard. The existence of grief, loss, trauma, tragedy and injustice, on top of the daily grind, are unavoidable realities. Even on a good day, there is usually something difficult happening too.

One of the ways we can practice caring for ourselves and increasing our capacity to navigate all of the challenges of life is to find ways to immerse ourselves in the beauty and goodness that life has to offer. When my soul is weary and I feel like I am going to fall apart, I have found that watching the sun's light cascade across the ocean with my feet nestled into the sand, turning on a song I love and dancing my heart out, or taking a long walk in a place with an abundance of trees puts me back together again.

For many years, I didn't do any of these things, and I suffered for it. I let busyness, guilt, and an incessant habit of putting other people's needs before my own prevent me from making time for the things that would bring me joy. It took me a long time to learn that self-care is not selfish. In fact it is an absolute necessity!

If we want to live healthy, balanced, thriving lives, it is so important that we create space to care for ourselves by doing the things that are life-giving, replenishing, refreshing or simply nurturing to us.

REFLECT

What activities are life-giving or nurturing for you? What brings you joy or rest? Explore the list below or come up with your own. If you aren't sure, pick a couple that you might want to try.

CAMPING	PLAYING GAMES
COLORING	PLAYING SPORTS
COOKING/BAKING	PRACTICING YOGA
DANCING	PURSUING NEW ADVENTURES
EXERCISING	READING
GARDENING	SCULPTING
HIKING	SINGING
JOURNALING	SPENDING TIME IN NATURE
LISTENING TO MUSIC	SPENDING TIME WITH FRIENDS
MAKING ART	TRAVELING
MAKING THINGS WITH MY HANDS	TRYING NEW THINGS
MEDITATING	VISITING MUSEUMS
NAPPING	VOLUNTEERING
PAINTING	WRITING
PAMPERING	

MY HEART COMES ALIVE WHEN I...

Write down the things that are life-giving or nurturing to you in the spaces below.

When you think about making time for one or more of the things that are life-giving or nurturing to you, what feelings come up for you?

What might prevent you from doing one of these activities? Can you see a solution to this barrier(s)?

Will you make time to do at least one thing that you believe will be life-giving or nurturing to you in the next week?

☐ I commit! ☐ I will do my best!

What Keeps You Grounded?
RESILIENCE BUILDING BLOCK: COPING

> "When all you know is fight or flight, red flags and butterflies *all feel the same.*"
>
> Cindy Cherie

To this day, if I am alone on an elevator and a man steps in to join me, my heart starts racing and I can feel my whole body tense up. My reaction has eased up over the years, but nevertheless, these feelings persist.

Something about being alone on an elevator with a man feels threatening to me. Whether or not I am in any real danger, my body *thinks* I am in danger and automatically reacts accordingly.

Bottom line, I am triggered.

Our bodies are wild and complex. When there is danger (real or perceived), our bodies' nervous systems are designed to protect us with automatic reactions. Typically, we respond in one of these ways:

Fight:
We move towards the threat aggressively.

Can feel like:
Agitated, angry, rigid

Freeze:
We find ourselves unable to move at all.

Can feel like:
Numb, helpless, hopeless, shut down.

Flight:
We move away from the threat.

Can feel like:
Pressured, speedy, anxious

Fawn:
The need to "please and appease" others in order to ensure safety.

Can feel like:
Shut down to self, hypervigilant toward the needs of others

We see this in nature too...

A mama bear aggressively protects her cubs from threat *(fight)*.

A gazelle runs from the threat of a lion *(flight)*.

A deer sees a car approaching and stops, frozen in its tracks *(freeze)*.

A dog rolls over and exposes their belly as a sign of submission *(fawn)*.

When we are feeling safe, we are more open, relaxed, and social. When we find ourselves flooded with overwhelming emotions or stress, we can use strategies known as grounding techniques to help us manage and regulate our response and calm our nervous system. Grounding techniques help us send a signal to our brains that lets our bodies know that we are safe.

The Goal Of Grounding

Our nervous systems are designed to alert us to danger. There are times when we truly need to fight, flee, freeze or fawn to survive or escape dangerous situations.

The goal of grounding techniques is NOT to try to make ourselves feel more safe in unsafe situations. For example, if you were crossing the street and suddenly saw a car driving right towards you, I would not advise that you pause to practice a deep breathing exercise in order to settle your nervous system. You would need to use every ounce of adrenaline you have to jump out of the way.

Grounding techniques are meant for those times when our bodies are telling us that we are in danger, even when we are not. For example, if someone really did get hit by a car while crossing a street, their nervous system might become activated every time they so much as saw a car, even when they were not in danger of being hit by one. Grounding techniques could help manage this overactive stress response.

PRACTICE

The tools below are grounding techniques that can help us cope when we are triggered. Check off the one(s) you want to try...

A Few Simple Grounding Techniques

- ☐ Run cold water over your hands or hold an ice cube for 30 seconds.

- ☐ Stop and scan your surroundings. Name 5 things you see in detail.

- ☐ Slow down your breathing. Try to make your exhale twice as long as your inhale for 3 breaths.

- ☐ Navy Seal Breathing/Box Breathing: Inhale for 4 seconds.

- ☐ Hold 4. Exhale 4. Repeat.

- ☐ Take a brisk walk or do jumping jacks.

PICK ONE YOU WANT TO PRACTICE NOW

1. BEFORE

Notice how you are feeling before you practice one of the grounding techniques above. What feelings are you experiencing? What do you notice in your body?

2. PRACTICE

Practice one of the grounding techniques above. Notice any feelings or sensations that come up for you during your practices and write them below.

3. AFTER

Notice how you are feeling after you practiced one of the grounding techniques above. What feelings are you experiencing? What do you notice in your body?

The next time I am feeling triggered and want to let my body know I am actually safe, I will....

(Name the grounding technique you plan to use)

Safety Check

If you are in an unsafe situation, we encourage you to get additional help.

Domestic Violence Hotline: 800-799-7233
National Trafficking Hotline: 888-373-7888

If you are in immediate danger, please call 911.

Dealing With Difficulties

RESILIENCE BUILDING BLOCK: COPING

> "Although the *world is full of suffering*, it is also full of the overcoming of it."
>
> — Helen Keller

One way or another, we need to find a way to deal with difficulties, stress and trauma.

Coping mechanisms are "the strategies people often use in the face of stress or trauma to help manage painful or difficult emotions.[6]"

Some coping mechanisms are conscious and intentional, others are subconscious and unintentional. In other words, sometimes we are aware of what we are doing in order to cope. Other times, we are unaware. We might find ourselves engaged in a certain behavior and not even realize what we are doing is a subconscious attempt to cope with hard things.

[6] https://www.goodtherapy.org/blog/psychpedia/coping-mechanisms

Coping mechanisms are designed to help us maintain a sense of emotional well-being in the face of emotional or physical tension. Experiences ranging from preparing for a job interview to chronic abuse produce a certain emotional or physical strain in us that we naturally find ways to cope with.

When I was in my twenties and involved in pimp-controlled stripping, I was in a lot of emotional pain, but I had made a vow to myself that I wouldn't cry. I told myself I needed to be strong. This helped me feel more in control.

The problem was, I had all of this pent up sadness and anger and no way of processing or expressing it. During this time, I began a habit of locking myself in the bathroom and tweezing my pubic hairs, one by one, for hours on end. I didn't see it then, but the ritual and pain of this distracted me from the emotional pain I was feeling. In short, I was coping.

Coping mechanisms can help us survive some really difficult situations. Some coping mechanisms are healthy and helpful. **These are called adaptive coping mechanisms.**

Other coping mechanisms might make us feel better in the short-term, but in the long-term, they may be harmful. **These are known as maladaptive coping mechanisms.**

Check out the lists below for examples of each type of coping mechanism.

ADAPTIVE COPING (Not harmful to ourselves or others)

- ☐ Relaxation: Meditation, prayer, grounding, deep breathing, etc.
- ☐ Talking to a Supportive Person
- ☐ Journaling or Expressive Writing
- ☐ Creative Expression: Dance, art, writing etc.
- ☐ Solution Seeking/Problem Solving
- ☐ Positive Reframing: Looking at problems in a more positive way. For example, viewing them as a challenge we have the capacity to face or even an opportunity.
- ☐ Physical Activity
- ☐ Humor
- ☐ Taking breaks
- ☐ Mindfulness
- ☐ Seeking support
- ☐ Other _____

MALADAPTIVE COPING (May offer short-term relief, but harmful in the long term)

- [ ] Escape: Isolation, withdrawal, or engaging in solitary activities such as watching TV, playing video games, scrolling, etc.
- [ ] Compulsive Risk-Taking: Adrenaline-seeking behaviors such as unsafe sex, gambling, or reckless driving.
- [ ] Substance Abuse
- [ ] Unhealthy Self-Soothing/Numbing: Such as overeating, binge drinking, substance abuse or excessive screen time.
- [ ] Self-Harm
- [ ] Blaming/Self-blame
- [ ] Shoplifting
- [ ] Unsafe Sex
- [ ] Avoidance
- [ ] Procrastination
- [ ] Worrying/Rumination
- [ ] Other _____

HOW DO YOU COPE?

Review the two lists of coping mechanisms above...check off the ones you have used to help you manage so far.

What do you notice about the coping mechanisms you highlighted?

Did you check anything on the second list? If so, welcome to the club! You are not alone. As humans, it is normal for us to find ways to cope with stress and trauma in our lives. One of the best ways to let go of a maladaptive coping mechanism is to replace it with a healthier one. This takes time, intention, and effort, but in the end you will be a healthier version of yourself with a greater capacity to manage hard things and thrive in life.

Which of the *adaptive* coping mechanisms above do you want to practice *more* in the next week?

Which of the *maladaptive* coping mechanisms above do you want to use *less* in the next week?

NO SHAME

Shame is not only unhelpful, it is damaging.

For any of you who are experiencing shame bubble to the surface as you contemplate maladapitve coping mechanisms, I want to invite you to release that shame. It is not only unhelpful, it can be damaging.

Guilt involves an awareness that we have done something inconsistent with our values. It can prompt us to right our wrongs and choose a different path. Shame, on the other hand, is the intensely painful experience of believing that you are fundamentally flawed.

Guilt says, "I *did* something bad".

Shame says, "I *am* bad".

When we entertain shame, it has a way of driving us deeper into pain and despair. When we find ourselves using maladaptive coping mechanisms, often we experience a sense of shame that only makes things worse. Frequently, our desire to cope with that shame drives us to repeat the very behavior we wish to stop.

If you find yourself engaging in maladaptive coping mechanisms, rather than entertaining shame, you can respond to yourself with compassion. For example, you can say to yourself,

"Wow, I must be in a lot of pain. I am doing XYZ."

This mindfulness and awareness is a first step in being able to shift your habits.

WHEN I NOTICE MYSELF...

NAME MALADAPTIVE COPING MECHANISM(S)

_____
_____
_____

I WILL SAY TO MYSELF...

WRITE THE COMPASSIONATE RESPONSE YOU WILL SAY TO YOURSELF

_____
_____
_____

Check Your Feelings

Now that you have completed a few more sections, it's time for another feelings check-in...

TOO MUCH TOO SOON?

If naming your feelings is too much too soon, you can circle one of the thumbs below that best describes your mood and move onto the next section.

Ready to name your feelings?

Using the chart below, circle which feeling(s) you are having...

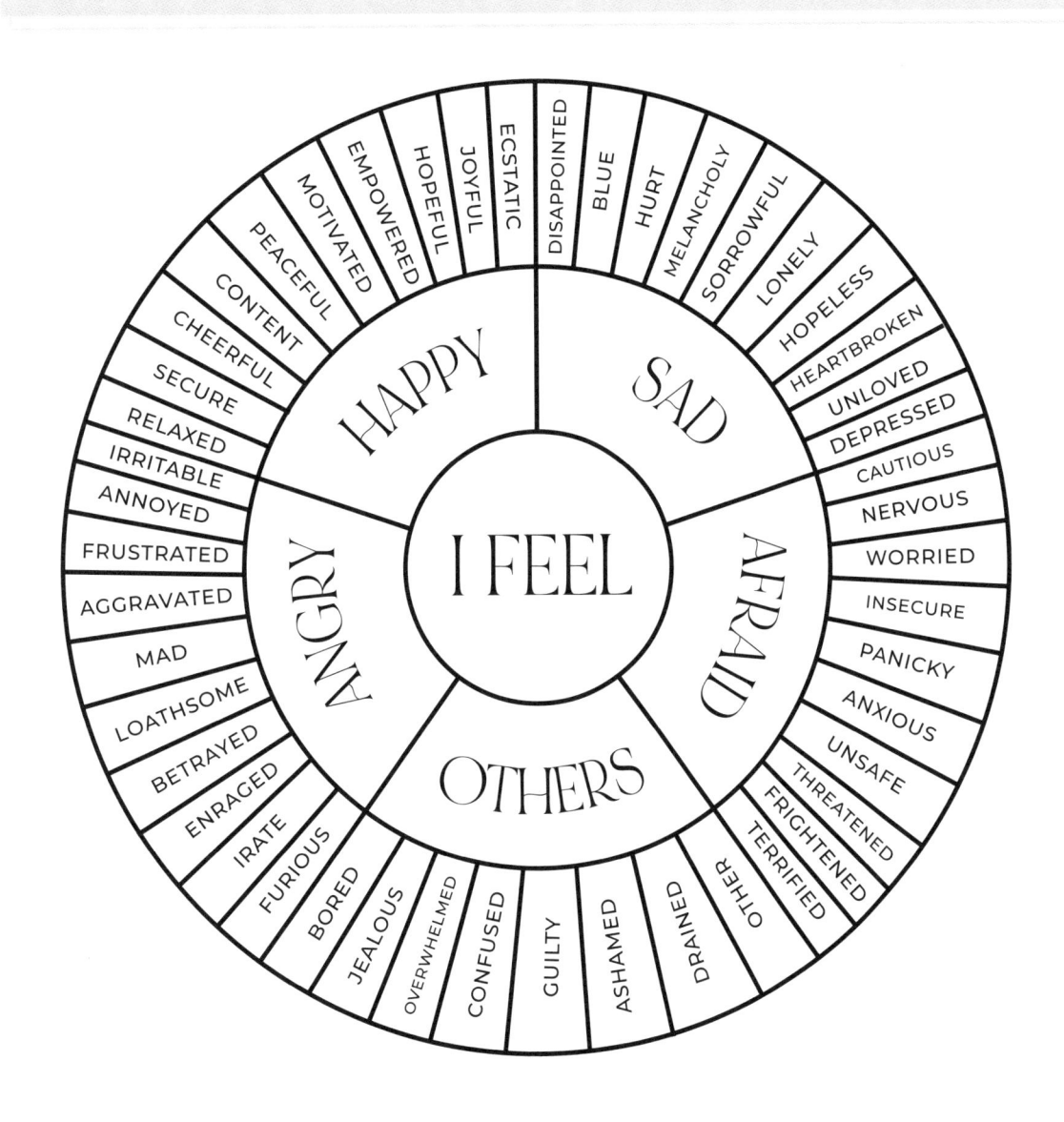

I FEEL

HAPPY: ECSTATIC, JOYFUL, HOPEFUL, EMPOWERED, MOTIVATED, PEACEFUL, CONTENT, CHEERFUL, SECURE, RELAXED

SAD: DISAPPOINTED, BLUE, HURT, MELANCHOLY, SORROWFUL, LONELY, HOPELESS, HEARTBROKEN, UNLOVED, DEPRESSED

AFRAID: CAUTIOUS, NERVOUS, WORRIED, INSECURE, PANICKY, ANXIOUS, UNSAFE, THREATENED, FRIGHTENED, TERRIFIED

OTHERS: OTHER, DRAINED, ASHAMED, GUILTY, CONFUSED, OVERWHELMED, JEALOUS, BORED

ANGRY: FURIOUS, IRATE, ENRAGED, BETRAYED, LOATHSOME, MAD, AGGRAVATED, FRUSTRATED, ANNOYED, IRRITABLE

What do you need?

Feelings are signals. They invite us to pay attention to what is happening around us and help dictate how we respond. Often, underneath our emotions are needs waiting to be met. The diagram below shows examples of this.

IF FEELINGS COULD TALK

SADNESS might be telling me i need **TO CRY**	**LONELINESS** might be telling me i need **CONNECTION**	**SHAME** might be telling me i need **SELF-COMPASSION**	**RESENTMENT** might be telling me i need **TO FORGIVE**
EMPTINESS might be telling me i need **TO DO SOMETHING CREATIVE**	**ANGER** might be telling me i need **TO CHECK-IN WITH MY BOUNDARIES**	**ANXIETY** might be telling me i need **TO BREATHE**	**STRESS** might be telling me i need **TO TAKE IT ONE STEP AT A TIME**

Illustration based on 'If Feelings Could Talk: A Free Social Emotional Learning Poster' by wholeheartedschoolcounseling.com

Based on how you are feeling right now, what do you need?

If you are feeling great, take a moment to celebrate this. If you are experiencing any difficult emotions, you might call someone on your support team or do something calming/uplifting like going for a walk. Refer to the diagram above for additional examples.

I FEEL

I NEED

What Is Love?

RESILIENCE BUILDING BLOCK: CONNECTION

> "Love falls to earth, rises from the ground, pools around the afflicted. Love pulls people back to their feet. Bodies and souls are fed. Bones and lives heal. New blades of grass grow from charred soil. *The sun rises.*"
>
> Anne Lamott

Leaving "the life" was hard. But leaving the relationship that had me stuck in "the life" was one of the hardest things I have ever done. I had known him since I was eleven years old. He had become the center of my world. At thirteen, when my mother left my 8-year-old brother and I alone for an entire summer, he was there for us. Buying us food and protecting us. I developed a deep belief that my survival depended on him.

When the relationship became emotionally and physically abusive, I stayed. This was all I had ever seen modeled to me, so I thought it was normal. *If all relationships are bad, why not try to make this one work?* I thought to myself. Besides that, every negative thing he said about me felt true. Having incredibly low self-esteem, his words validated what I already believed about myself.

That relationship ultimately led to me working in strip clubs. Each night, I came home and gave him all of my money. I didn't think of him as a pimp. He was my boyfriend. It was us against the world. I was determined that if I stuck it out, if I stayed long enough and fought hard enough, somehow, someway, things would get better and I would have my happy ending.*7

Part of the problem was, my whole life, people told me they loved me with their words. And yet, they rejected, neglected, abused and abandoned me with their actions.

We are designed to love and be loved. If our life is a seed, love is the soil, and the rain, and the sun. It is what makes us flourish. Of course, humans are imperfect beings that love imperfectly. But love, when it is true, creates a sense of safety and security and inspires us to become the best version of ourselves.

---

[7]*If you want to read my full story, check out my memoir, Scars and Stilettos.*

When I learned what true love actually looked like, it was a game-changer. I discovered the wisdom of an ancient writing that holds profound insight about love:

> *Love is large and incredibly patient. Love is gentle and consistently kind to all. It refuses to be jealous when blessing comes to someone else. Love does not brag about one's achievements nor inflate its own importance. Love does not traffic in shame and disrespect, nor selfishly seek its own honor. Love is not easily irritated or quick to take offense. Love joyfully celebrates honesty and finds no delight in what is wrong. Love is a safe place of shelter, for it never stops believing the best for others. Love never takes failure as defeat, for it never gives up.*
>
> **1 Corinthians 13:4-7 (TPT)**

I would like to invite you to participate in an activity using the writings above...

Think of someone you are in a relationship with. It would be best to choose the relationship that takes up most of your time and emotional energy. Now, read this paragraph again, but anytime you come across a reference to the word "love", replace it with the name of the person you are thinking of.

Love Is

_____ is large and incredibly patient. _____ is gentle and consistently kind to a_____ refuses to be jealous when blessing comes to someone else._____ does not brag about their achievements nor inflate their own importance._____ does not traffic in shame and disrespect, nor selfishly seek their own honor._____ not easily irritated or quick to take offense._____ joyfully celebrates honesty and finds no delight in what is wrong._____ a safe place of shelter, for they never stop believing the best for others. _____ never takes failure as defeat, for _____ never gives up.

1 Corinthians 13:4-7 (TPT)

REFLECT

When you reflect on the exercise above, what stands out to you?
Do these statements ring true?

Does the way the person treats you reflect this definition of love?
How does the answer to this question make you feel?

Do you believe you deserve this type of love? Where do you think that belief might come from?

Are there any areas where you recognize that you can also grow in your expression of love? If so, name them.

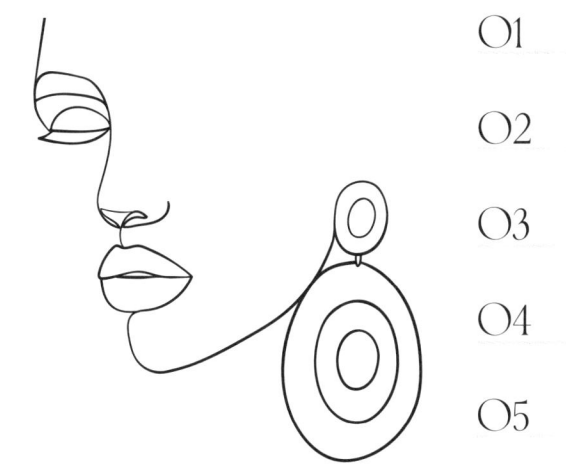

O1

O2

O3

O4

O5

I loved my exploiter. More than anything, I wanted to believe he loved me too. But when I place his name in the sentences above, it is clear to me that what he had to offer me was not love. Instead, he was unkind, impatient, easily angered, jealous, prideful, dishonoring, and self-seeking.

I have discovered that love is a verb. When people say they love us, we can look beyond their words and examine their actions. If what someone tells you does not match up with what they show you, believe what they show you because that is the truth of who they really are.

Of course, none of us is capable of loving perfectly. But if the way you are being treated consistently falls short of love, it is worth paying attention to. It is likely a reflection of their character, not your lovability.

One of my favorite quotes of all time is a helpful reminder of this...

> *When someone shows you who they are.*
> *Believe them the first time.*
>
> **Maya Angelou**

Check Your Feelings

Now that you have completed a few more sections, it's time for another feelings check-in...

TOO MUCH TOO SOON?

If naming your feelings is too much too soon, you can circle one of the thumbs below that best describes your mood and move onto the next section.

Ready to name your feelings?

Using the chart below, circle which feeling(s) you are having...

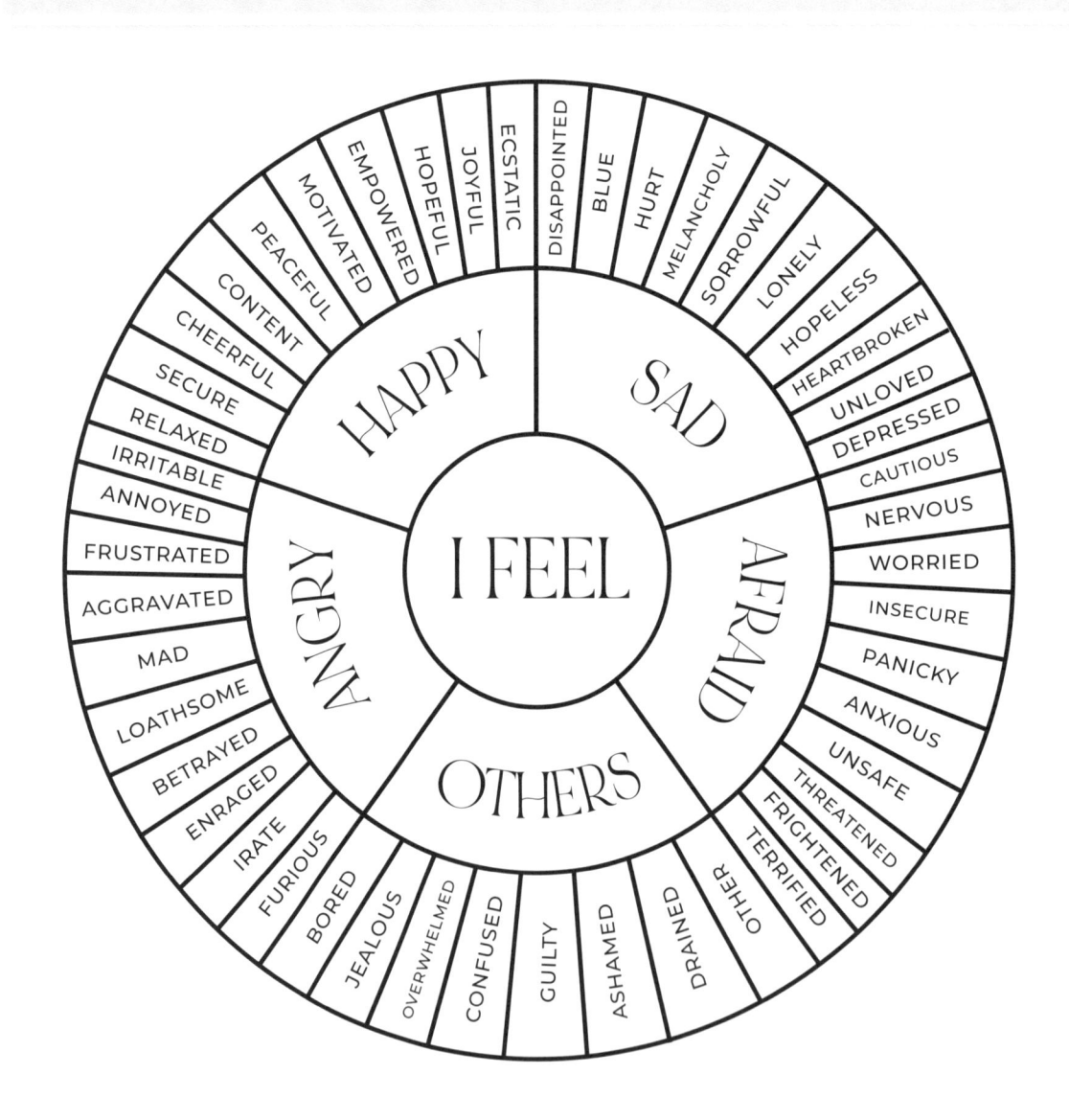

I FEEL

- **HAPPY**: ecstatic, joyful, hopeful, empowered, motivated, peaceful, content, cheerful, secure, relaxed
- **SAD**: disappointed, blue, hurt, melancholy, sorrowful, lonely, hopeless, heartbroken, unloved, depressed
- **AFRAID**: cautious, nervous, worried, insecure, panicky, anxious, unsafe, threatened, frightened, terrified
- **ANGRY**: irritable, annoyed, frustrated, aggravated, mad, loathsome, betrayed, enraged, irate, furious
- **OTHERS**: bored, jealous, overwhelmed, confused, guilty, ashamed, drained, other

What do you need?

Feelings are signals. They invite us to pay attention to what is happening around us and help dictate how we respond. Often, underneath our emotions are needs waiting to be met. The diagram below shows examples of this.

IF FEELINGS COULD TALK

SADNESS might be telling me i need **TO CRY**	**LONELINESS** might be telling me i need **CONNECTION**	**SHAME** might be telling me i need **SELF-COMPASSION**	**RESENTMENT** might be telling me i need **TO FORGIVE**
EMPTINESS might be telling me i need **TO DO SOMETHING CREATIVE**	**ANGER** might be telling me i need **TO CHECK-IN WITH MY BOUNDARIES**	**ANXIETY** might be telling me i need **TO BREATHE**	**STRESS** might be telling me i need **TO TAKE IT ONE STEP AT A TIME**

Illustration based on 'If Feelings Could Talk: A Free Social Emotional Learning Poster' by wholeheartedschoolcounseling.com

Based on how you are feeling right now, what do you need?

If you are feeling great, take a moment to celebrate this. If you are experiencing any difficult emotions, you might call someone on your support team or do something calming/uplifting like going for a walk. Refer to the diagram above for additional examples.

I FEEL

I NEED

Boundaries

RESILIENCE BUILDING BLOCKS: COMPETENCE, CONFIDENCE, CONNECTION, CHARACTER AND CONTROL

> "*No* is a *complete* sentence..."
>
> Unknown

I used to be a people-pleaser to the max. One of my best survival strategies growing up in a chaotic household was keeping the people around me happy by being cheerful and agreeable. If you remember what we covered in "What Keeps You Grounded" and are thinking this sounds like a "fawn" response, you are right!

I tried to control the emotional tone of my home with an upbeat attitude. When it came to my exploiter, I used the same strategy: Please and appease. In the strip clubs, people-pleasing was the job description and "no" wasn't a word I got to say very often.

In many ways, pleasing and appeasing helped me to adapt and survive. But as I got older, it was no longer serving me.

Saying "yes" to one thing means we are saying "no" to something else. My incessant need to people-please and my fear of telling people "no" meant that I allowed my life to revolve completely around the wants, needs, and feelings of others. There was no room for "me" in my own life. I said "yes" to allowing myself to get sucked into drama, chaos, and even abuse. This meant I was essentially saying "no" to things like self-care, emotional honesty, and healthy boundaries.

Including "no" in my vocabulary has been an incredibly empowering experience.

> *"No, I will not drop everything to 'rescue' you every time your life spins out of control."*
> *"No, I won't be able to work your shift again and give up my one day off."*
> *"No, I will not continue to engage in a conversation with you when you talk to me that way."*
> *"No, as much as I would like to accept your invitation, I will not be able to make it this time."*

In many cases, we don't even need to back up our "no" with a reason. **No is a complete sentence;** It is not the beginning of a negotiation. We don't need to help people accept our "no" by giving them lengthy explanations. Healthy people who care about you are going to accept your "no" without all of the added excuses.

Learning about healthy boundaries has been one of the most life-changing elements of my journey to healing and freedom.

While learning to say "no" is a key component of boundaries, having healthy boundaries goes beyond simply being able to say "no." Boundaries are the limits we put in place to protect our well being.

They determine who we are and who we are not, what we will tolerate and what we will not. They establish where we end and where the other person begins.

A thriving life requires healthy boundaries.

BOUNDARIES DEFINE

Who we are	Who we are **NOT**
What we will do	What we will **NOT** do
What we will tolerate	What we will **NOT** tolerate

HOMES

Before we dig deeper into boundaries, I would like to invite you to participate in an activity... As you think about boundaries, spend some time looking through the photos below. Choose one photo that you are drawn to or that stands out to you.

REFLECT

What drew you to the picture you chose?

What do you notice about this photo?

FENCES & WALLS

One of my favorite books on the planet is Boundaries, by Cloud and Townsend. To help illustrate the concept of boundaries, the authors refer to boundaries as fences—physical property lines that establish where our property begins and ends. Ultimately, we are responsible for what happens on our property, just as we are responsible for our own lives.

I spent a lot of years, especially in romantic relationships, with no fence at all. Because I had no clearly established boundaries, others found it easy to take advantage of me. Often, this would go on until I finally got fed up and threw up a giant impenetrable wall, pushing them out completely. Sometimes, after enough time had passed or they offered up an apology, I would bring down the wall and let them back in, even though they hadn't done anything to earn back my trust. A therapist once referred to this as the "all or nothing wall."

As it turns out, I knew how to either let people all the way into my heart and life without any regard for the impact their actions were having on me, or how to push them all the way out. There was no in between. No fence. No clearly communicated boundaries. When we don't know how to put up a fence to protect ourselves, we might end up falling into this "all or nothing wall" pattern.

Here are some benefits to having a fence (aka boundaries):

• If someone barges through my fence, ignoring my boundary, it shows me they are unsafe and a bigger boundary is needed.

• Fences don't prevent relationships and intimacy like walls do. They allow space for these things, while maintaining boundaries.

• I can invite someone into my yard for a visit. If they build trust with me by showing me they respect my property/boundaries, perhaps I can invite them onto my porch and eventually into my home. But I am still the owner of my own property. They can't start bringing in their own furniture, redecorating my living room or using my yard as their personal dumping ground. If they were to do this, I would ask them to remove themselves from my property and would not let them in again unless trust was built and there was clear evidence of change.

REFLECT

Does the idea of boundaries as fences and the all or nothing wall impact the way you view the photo you were initially drawn to? If so, how? What else do you notice about the photo you chose?

Does the picture you selected communicate anything to you about your own boundaries? Please describe...

SIGNS SOMEONE DOESN'T RESPECT YOUR BOUNDARIES

As I mentioned before, healthy people will accept your boundaries. People who really love you will also love your boundaries. So, how do we know when our boundaries are not being respected? Check out the signs in the list below and circle the ones you have experienced...

YOU

- START DOUBTING YOUR BOUNDARIES
- SENSE SOMETHING IS OFF
- MAKE EXCUSES ON THEIR BEHAVIOR
- LET THEM CONVINCE YOU OTHERWISE
- YOU FEEL GUILTY ABOUT YOUR BOUNDARIES
- GIVE YOU A GUILT TRIP

THEY

- DISREGARD YOUR DECISIONS
- TRY TO MANIPULATE YOU
- PUNISH YOU FOR YOUR BOUNDARY
- PRESSURE YOU
- IGNORE YOUR BOUNDARY

Have you ever experienced a time when your boundaries were not being respected? How did you respond?

If you were faced with the same situation today, would you respond differently? If so, how?

As you reflect on this list of signs someone doesn't respect your boundaries, are there any people currently in your life that demonstrate a lack of respect for your boundaries?

☐ Yes
☐ No

WHEN COMMUNICATING BOUNDARIES ISN'T SAFE

In order to set a healthy boundary, two things are necessary. We need to be safe and we need to be able to operate out of choice.

Many of us have experienced situations where we were unsafe and perhaps or our agency/ability to choose was not respected. THIS IS NOT OUR FAULT.

Please know, there are some situations or relationships that are so unsafe, the only appropriate boundary is to cut off the relationship and all communication with them entirely. This means you do not even communicate your boundary with them; you simply set it. If you are in an unsafe situation, call 911 or contact one of the hotlines at the end of this section.

3 KEYS TO BOUNDARIES

In order for boundaries to be truly effective, there are three keys necessary.

1. Know your boundaries
2. Communicate your boundaries
3. Follow through on consequences when boundaries are crossed

Knowing our boundaries is the first critical step in setting them. But people aren't mind readers. So, it isn't enough for us to simply know our boundaries, we also need to be able to communicate them. Once we have communicated our boundary, it is up to us to enforce it. A boundary is only truly a boundary if it has a consequence.

LET'S PRACTICE

EXAMPLE
Describe Your Boundary:

I will not tolerate yelling or name-calling.

Provide some examples of how you might communicate your boundaries:

1. If you want to continue to have this conversation, I need you to lower your voice.

2. I am not comfortable with the way you are speaking to me. I need you to stop.

3. I will not allow you to continue to speak to me that way. If you continue, I will (insert consequence).

What will the consequences be if someone doesn't respect your boundary?

1. I will hang up the phone.

2. I will walk away/leave the situation.

3. I will set limits around how frequently I speak to them and/or what topics I discuss with them.

YOUR TURN

> **EXAMPLE**
> Describe Your Boundary:

_____
_____

Provide some examples of how you might communicate your boundaries:

O1 _____

O2 _____

O3 _____

What will the consequences be if someone doesn't respect your boundary?

O1 _____

O2 _____

O3 _____

Setting a new boundary with someone who doesn't respect our boundaries can be hard. *Really hard.*

Often, people who are used to being able to violate our boundaries become frustrated and even angry at us. They may even throw a tantrum about it. (Not joking!)

If you are experiencing resistance to boundaries with someone in your life, this might be a good time to enlist the help of someone you identified in your support system.

Safety Check

If you are in an unsafe situation, we encourage you to get additional help.

Domestic Violence Hotline: 800-799-7233
National Trafficking Hotline: 888-373-7888

If you are in immediate danger, please call 911.

Check Your Feelings

Now that you have completed a few more sections, it's time for another feelings check-in...

TOO MUCH TOO SOON?

If naming your feelings is too much too soon, you can circle one of the thumbs below that best describes your mood and move onto the next section.

Ready to name your feelings?

Using the chart below, circle which feeling(s) you are having...

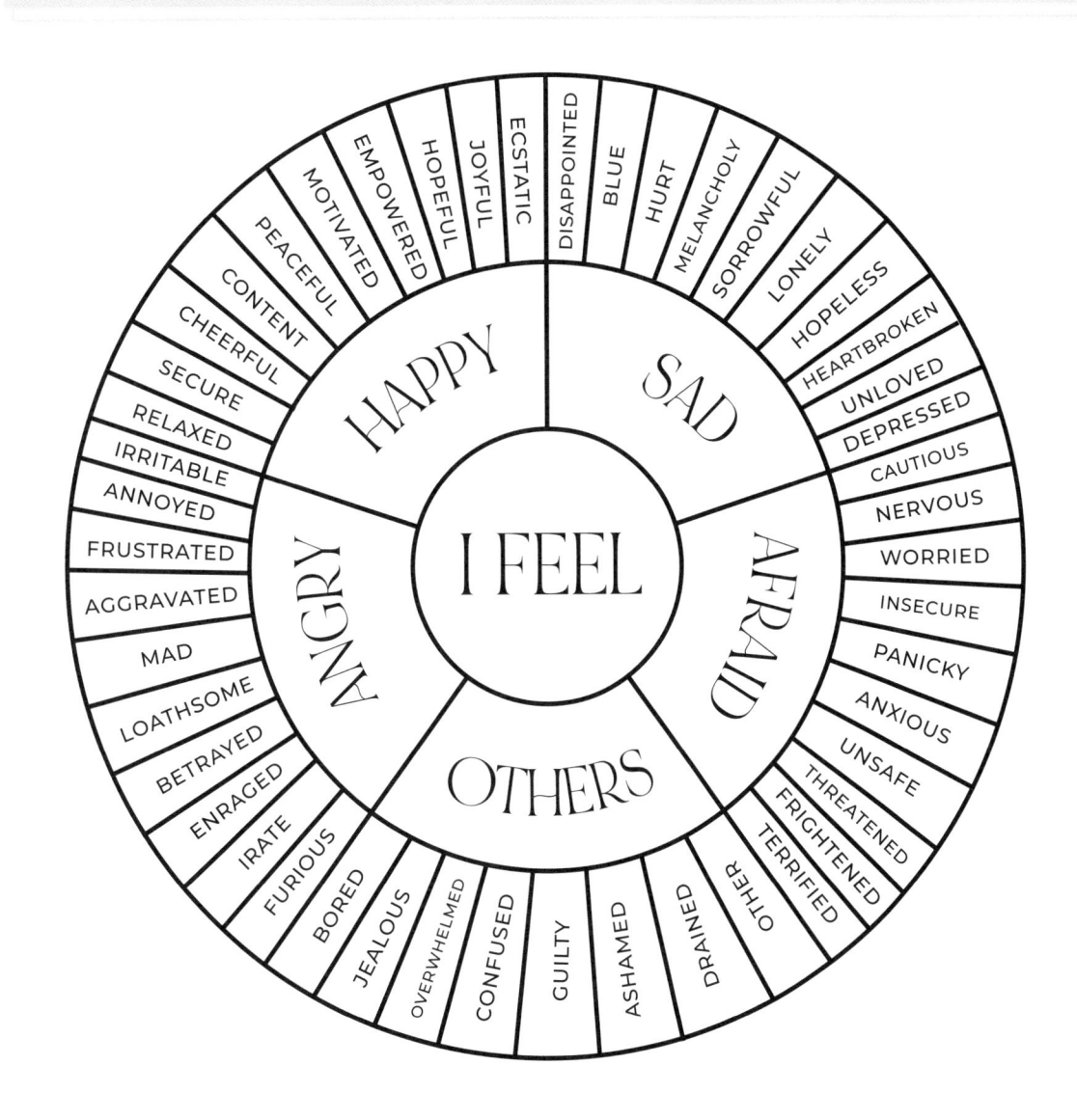

I FEEL

- **HAPPY**: ECSTATIC, JOYFUL, HOPEFUL, EMPOWERED, MOTIVATED, PEACEFUL, CONTENT, CHEERFUL, SECURE, RELAXED
- **SAD**: DISAPPOINTED, BLUE, HURT, MELANCHOLY, SORROWFUL, LONELY, HOPELESS, HEARTBROKEN, UNLOVED, DEPRESSED
- **AFRAID**: CAUTIOUS, NERVOUS, WORRIED, INSECURE, PANICKY, ANXIOUS, UNSAFE, THREATENED, FRIGHTENED, TERRIFIED
- **OTHERS**: OTHER, DRAINED, ASHAMED, GUILTY, CONFUSED, OVERWHELMED, JEALOUS, BORED
- **ANGRY**: FURIOUS, IRATE, ENRAGED, BETRAYED, LOATHSOME, MAD, AGGRAVATED, FRUSTRATED, ANNOYED, IRRITABLE

What do you need?

Feelings are signals. They invite us to pay attention to what is happening around us and help dictate how we respond. Often, underneath our emotions are needs waiting to be met. The diagram below shows examples of this.

IF FEELINGS COULD TALK

SADNESS might be telling me i need **TO CRY**	**LONELINESS** might be telling me i need **CONNECTION**	**SHAME** might be telling me i need **SELF-COMPASSION**	**RESENTMENT** might be telling me i need **TO FORGIVE**
EMPTINESS might be telling me i need **TO DO SOMETHING CREATIVE**	**ANGER** might be telling me i need **TO CHECK-IN WITH MY BOUNDARIES**	**ANXIETY** might be telling me i need **TO BREATHE**	**STRESS** might be telling me i need **TO TAKE IT ONE STEP AT A TIME**

Illustration based on 'If Feelings Could Talk: A Free Social Emotional Learning Poster' by wholeheartedschoolcounseling.com

Based on how you are feeling right now, what do you need?

If you are feeling great, take a moment to celebrate this. If you are experiencing any difficult emotions, you might call someone on your support team or do something calming/uplifting like going for a walk. Refer to the diagram above for additional examples.

I FEEL

I NEED

Core Values

RESILIENCE BUILDING BLOCKS: CHARACTER

> "Values are like fingerprints. Nobody's are the same, but you leave 'em all over *everything* you do."
>
> Elvis Presley

The first thing I ever stole was a lip gloss from the Slauson Swap Meet in what was then known as South Central, LA. My friends and I put on matching outfits. Black biker shorts with white t-shirts adorned with black sharpie marker. The song Lean on Me by Bill Withers was playing in heavy rotation on KJLH (Don't judge me because I am old. That is ageism). Paying homage to the song, we wrote "Lean. On. Me." on our respective shirts. We put on our little gold door knocker earrings and strutted down Crenshaw Boulevard like we were J.J. Fad. If you don't know them, do yourself a favor and look up Supersonic. They are female hip hop legends.

The only thing we needed to complete our look was a purple lip gloss that was popular at the time. The problem was, none of us had the $1.99 to pay for it ourselves. My friends told me I would have to be the one to steal it since I am white and would be less likely to get caught. Sadly, they were right. In all of my years of shoplifting that followed, I never once got caught. Meanwhile, my friends were being hauled off to juvie. But that is a whole other story.

After that, when my mom left my brother and I that summer, I used my newfound shoplifting skills to steal food from the liquor store in order to feed us. Soon, my exploiter capitalized on my "talents", periodically forcing me to steal money and run scams. By the time he had me in strip clubs, hustling was a way of life.

When I left my pimp and the sex industry, once again I was short on money and groceries. So I started running a scam to get food. I thought it was pretty harmless because the only ones being cheated were big corporations and they had lots of money anyway. At least that is how I rationalized it.

One day I called my aunt and offhandedly mentioned how I got my hands on a bunch of groceries that week.

"Harmony, what if your Auntie Krissi owned that company? Would you still think that was okay?"

The moment she said it, I realized that since leaving "the life", I had come to value integrity, however, I was not operating within my values. After that awakening, I never stole or scammed again.

Our personal core values act as a compass, guiding our decisions, actions, and behaviors. They reflect our highest priorities and our most fundamental beliefs. When we are aware of our values, we have a clear sense of what is important to us, what we stand for, and what we want to achieve in life.

This clarity provides a sense of purpose, direction, and meaning, which contributes to a greater sense of fulfillment and well-being.

By identifying and living according to our values, we align our actions with our authentic self. This alignment promotes a sense of self-integrity.

Our values can become a driving force in our lives. When we live in a way that is consistent with our values, it brings peace.

When we act outside of our values, we can use that as an opportunity to realign ourselves with our values and course-correct.

CORE VALUES

> Review the list below and underline any core values that resonate with you.

ACHIEVEMENT	CREATIVITY	HUMILITY
ADAPTABILITY	CURIOSITY	HUMOR
ADVENTURE	DETERMINATION	INDEPENDENCE
AFFECTION	EDUCATION	INFLUENCE
AUTHENTICITY	EMPATHY	INTEGRITY
AUTHORITY	FAIRNESS	JUSTICE
AUTONOMY	FAITH	KINDNESS
BALANCE	FAME	KNOWLEDGE
BEAUTY	FAMILY	LEADERSHIP
BOLDNESS	FLEXIBILITY	LEARNING
CAREER	FRIENDSHIPS	LOVE
COMMITMENT	FUN	LOYALTY
COMMUNITY	GENEROSITY	MATURITY
COMPASSION	GROWTH	MEANINGFUL WORK
CONTRIBUTION	HAPPINESS	OPENNESS
COURAGE	HONESTY	OPTIMISM

PEACE	RESPECT	STABILITY
POPULARITY	RESPONSIBILITY	SUCCESS
POWER	SECURITY	TRUSTWORTHINESS
PRESTIGE	SELF-IMPROVEMENT	WEALTH
RECOGNITION	SELF-RESPECT	WISDOM
RELIGION	SERVICE	OTHER_____
REPUTATION	SPIRITUALITY	

Once you have underlined all of the values in the list above that resonate with you, go back through and decide on your top 3-5 core values. Write them in the spaces of the diamond below.

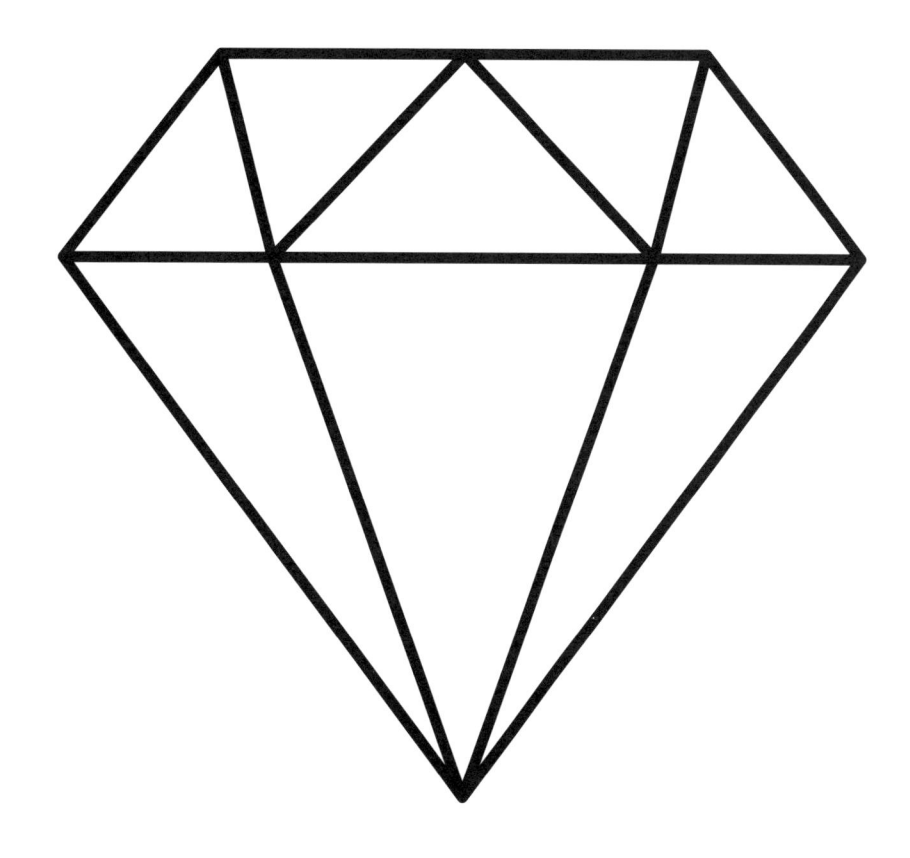

REFLECT

Overall, do you believe your life reflects your core values? Please describe.

Is there anything in your life that you might want to adjust in order to become more aligned with your core values?

THE LIFE YOU WANT

RESILIENCE BUILDING BLOCKS: COMPETENCE AND CONTROL

> "The only way to get to where you are going is to *start where you are.*"
>
> Harmony Dust

I want you to dream and I want you to dream big. I want you to imagine the beautiful, expansive and thriving life you are meant to live. I also want you to actually live it. And I believe you can.

One day at a time, one step at a time, starting right where you are.

Chances are, the journey to your best life will require stepping out of your comfort zone. It will involve learning new skills, taking new risks, and ultimately, spending time intentionally developing one or more areas of your life.

That process starts with bravely assessing where you are today. Taking an honest and holistic look at your life can help you determine where you may need to build and grow in order to achieve your dreams.

I quit making New Year's resolutions 15 years ago. Before that, I was still deeply struggling with body image issues and a history of disordered eating. Most of the time, "lose weight" topped the list of my resolutions. January 1st usually marked the start of whatever diet craze was most popular at the time. Aside from my never-ending weight loss resolutions, most years, I was making commitments to superficial goals that had little to do with creating a meaningful, thriving life.

Today, I am much more concerned with who I am becoming and what kind of life I want to live than the number on the scale or setting lofty, unattainable goals that I will probably give up on by March.

Now, at the start of each year, I engage in a practice of honestly examining the most important areas of my life, deciding what areas may need attention and creating a realistic, achievable plan as to how I want to spend my time and energy in the following year. I have found this practice to be pretty life-changing. Not in an instantaneous way, but in the way that lasting change often happens—slow and steady, one step at a time.

WHEEL OF LIFE

The Wheel of Life is a visual tool that can help you assess your life's balance as well as your overall satisfaction with where you are. It can also help you determine what areas of your life might need some extra love and attention.

CREATING A WHEEL OF LIFE

STEP 01

Identify the most important areas of your life. Here are some examples you may want to consider:

FAMILY	ENVIRONMENT (HOME OR WORK)
FRIENDSHIPS/COMMUNITY	PERSONAL GROWTH
ROMANCE/PARTNERSHIP	FUN AND RECREATION
CAREER/WORK	LIVING SITUATION
SPIRITUALITY	MENTAL/EMOTIONAL HEALTH
FINANCES/MONEY	EDUCATION/LEARNING
HEALTH	COMMUNICATION

STEP 02

Add your top 8 categories as labels for the sections of your wheel.

The concept was originally created by Paul J. Meyer, founder of Success Motivation

STEP 03

Rank your level of satisfaction with each category by marking the number on the scale. With 1 being extremely dissatisfied and 10 being extremely satisfied.

STEP 04

Draw a line to connect each of the points on your graph. Your diagram might look like the one below.

STEP 05

Reflect on your Wheel of Life.

EXAMPLE

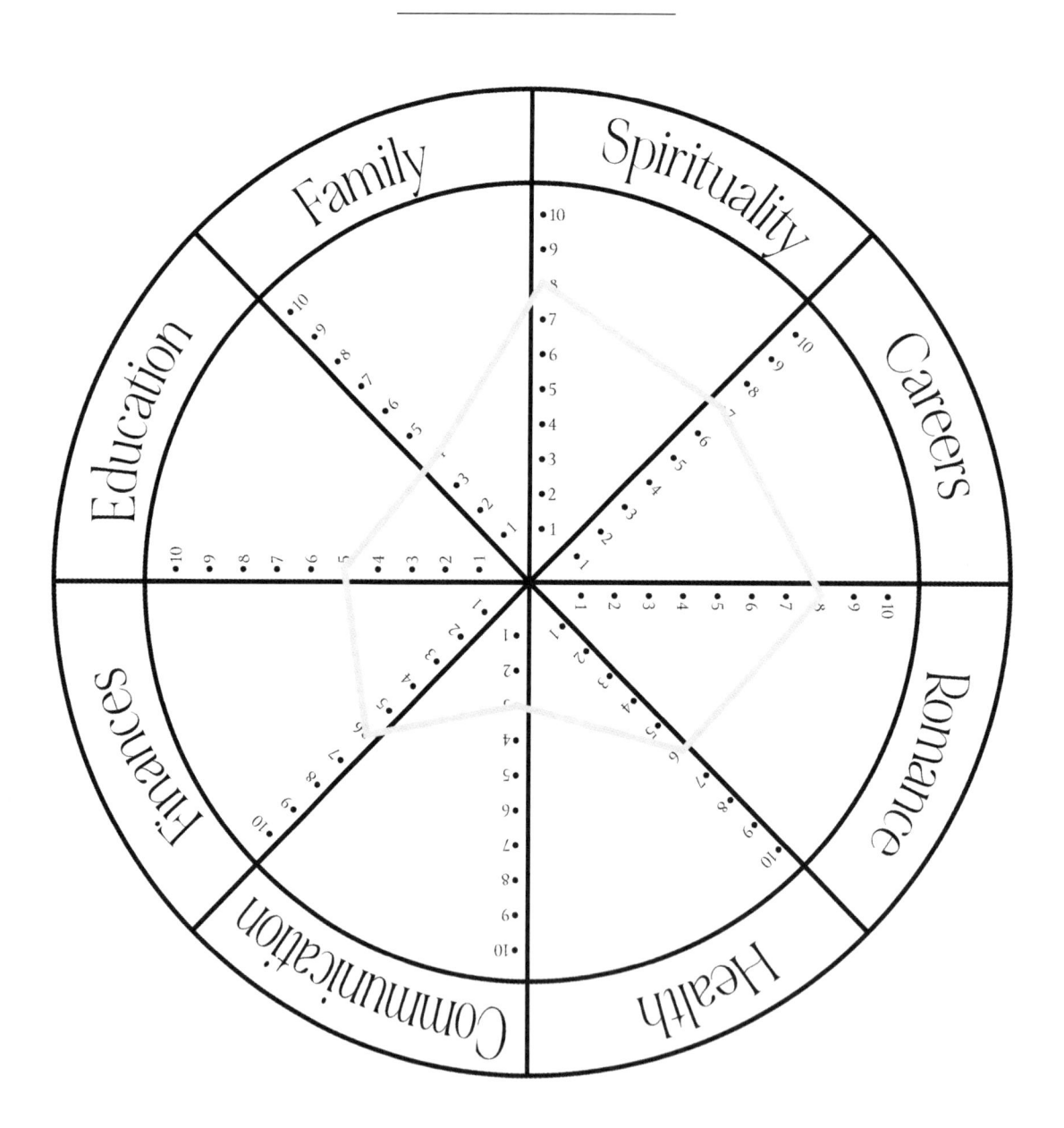

YOUR TURN

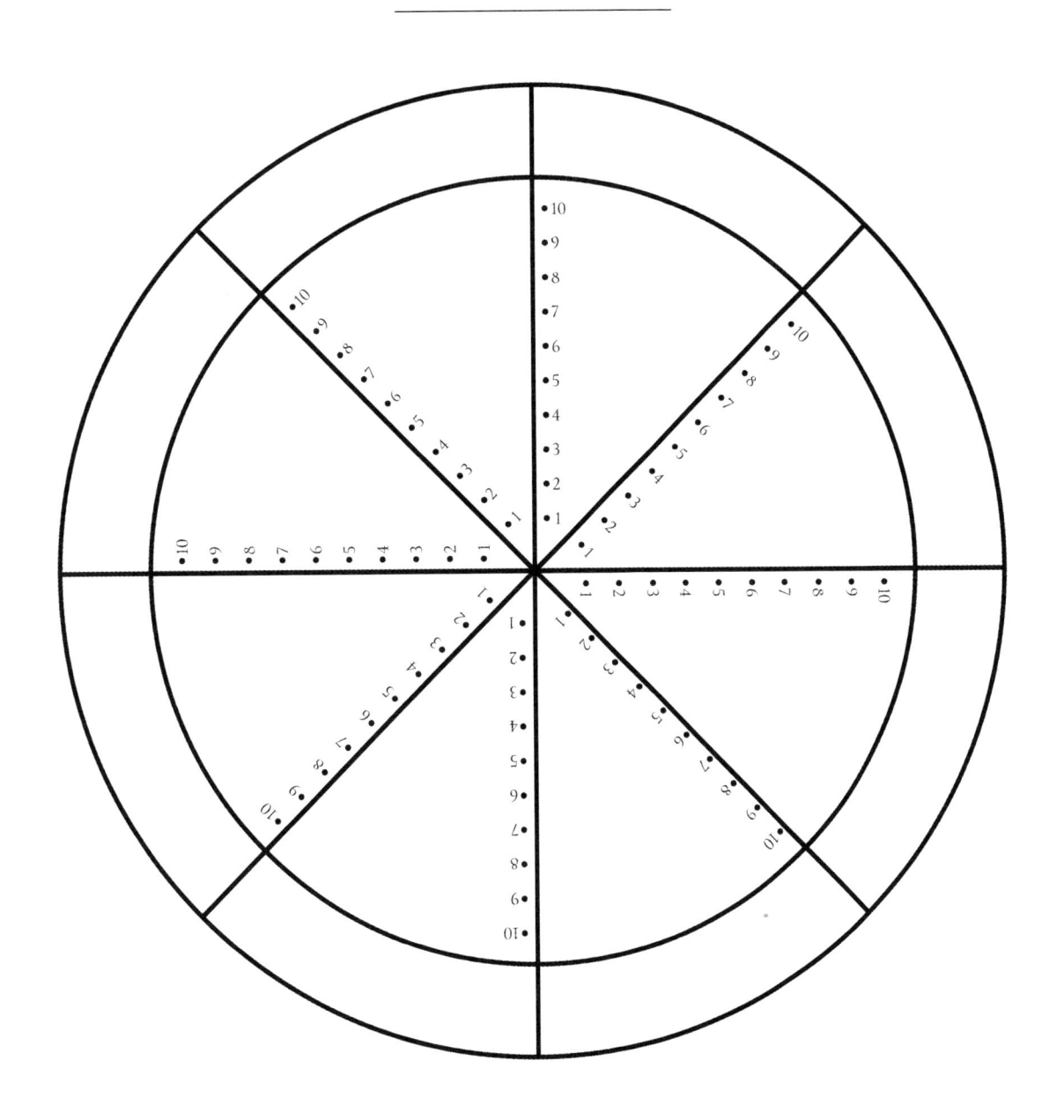

REFLECT

Depending on where we are at, it can be overwhelming to take an honest look at our lives. Some of you may have found that activity fun, insightful, and inspiring. For others, seeing your life satisfaction mapped out so clearly may bring up feelings of grief or frustration.

As you reflect on your Wheel of Life, I encourage you to respond to yourself with compassion and kindness. You are here. You are showing up for yourself and doing the work.
You can be proud of that.

> What thoughts or feelings come up for you as you review your Wheel of Life?

What surprises you the most about your
Wheel of Life?

When you look at the web-like shape that appears when you connect the points on your wheel, what stands out to you?

Which area would you most like to see strengthened
or improved?

Which area would you like to start with?

What small step would have the most significant impact on your satisfaction with that area of your life?

FREE TO DREAM

RESILIENCE BUILDING BLOCK: CONTROL AND CONTRIBUTION

> "Tell me, what is it you plan to do with your one *wild and precious* life?"
>
> Mary Oliver

When I tell my story, I often share about the time when I was 13-years-old and my mother left me with my 8-year-old brother to fend for ourselves for three months. You may even remember me mentioning it here in this workbook. She handed me $20 and a book of food stamps before she left. It was that summer that I became involved with an older boy in the neighborhood who preyed on my vulnerability and eventually became my pimp.

This is the story that I tell about my mother. Again and again. But my mother was so much more than a soundbite in my story.

There were so many seasons of her, so many versions of her.

She believed in the importance of imagination and playing in dirt. She liked floppy ears and silly faces. Fairies and frogs and polka-dotted mushrooms. The child in her remained quite accessible on her good days.

She sat on porches, admiring the moon and its many faces, puffing on Benson and Hedges or American Spirits, depending on the decade.

She took us on night hikes and road trips. She taught us to fight for justice and told us it backfired when we were old enough to stand up to her.

She encouraged us to use our voices and to tell the truth. She supported me, even when I began using my voice to tell the hard parts of our truth.

She rescued broken-winged sparrows and crows. And sometimes she tried to do this with people too.

She wrote poems about the selves she wanted to be and the selves she wanted to let go of. Poems about generations. Poems about us.

She made mugwort tea and turquoise jewelry. She made lasagna and cake with cream-cheese frosting for our birthdays.

She also made mistakes. Because, as I came to realize, she wasn't just a mom— she was a person too. Doing the best she could with what she had, just like the rest of us.

And she always, always told me I could change the world.

Eventually, I believed her.

At the age of 22, my newfound faith inspired me to believe that I was, indeed, created with a purpose. This realization watered the seed my mother had planted deep in my heart. One night, standing in a table dance booth at the strip club with a man gazing at all of me—a man whose name I will never know—it hit me...

"If I was created with a purpose, surely this can't be it."

This revelation became the catalyst for change in my life. It was many years before I began to see the purpose for my life take shape. But that night, in an LA strip club, my journey of pursuing purpose began.

The most miraculous part is, those things that I thought would hold me back or disqualify me from a life of purpose have become the very things that have propelled me into my purpose. In 2003, five years after leaving the abusive and exploitative relationship with my pimp, I found myself parked across the street from the strip club where I used to work. I wondered about my old coworkers. Had they moved on to other clubs, or other lives, or were they still there?

I remembered that life: the suffocating feeling of being trapped with no end in sight; wanting the money, needing it, but wishing there were some other legal way to get it. The constant pressure to smile and pretend you want nothing more than to fulfill every wish and fantasy of a stranger, when all you really want to do is lie around your apartment in sweatpants, watching mafia movies like Goodfellas and Casino – imagining you could live some other life.

I remembered, and all I could do was pray. And it was right there in my green Honda Civic that the vision of Treasures was birthed—a dream to provide outreach and support to women who have experienced exploitation and trafficking. Every day, I get to see the pain from my past used to inspire others to heal and grow and move towards thriving lives.

I believe, with everything in me, you were created for a purpose. Maybe you believe that too and that seed of destiny inside of you has already been activated. Or maybe you are like so many of the women I sit with and you aren't so sure. In either case, my desire is that these questions will stir hope, ignite vision, and inspire purpose in you.

REFLECT

What makes you come alive?

01 _____

02 _____

03 _____

04 _____

05 _____

What keeps you up at night?

If money were no obstacle, how would you like to spend your time?

What do you enjoy talking about?

Name three things you are good at.

What job did you dream of doing when you were a child?

What were you passionate about as a child/teen? Are you still passionate about any of these things?

If you could take a class on anything, what would it be?

Has there been a time when you felt a sense of purpose? If so, what were you doing?

What injustices in the world would you like to see changed?

Who do you admire? What about them do you admire?

How do you want to be remembered?

Check Your Feelings

Now that you have completed a few more sections, it's time for another feelings check-in...

TOO MUCH TOO SOON?

If naming your feelings is too much too soon, you can circle one of the thumbs below that best describes your mood and move onto the next section.

Ready to name your feelings?

Using the chart below, circle which feeling(s) you are having...

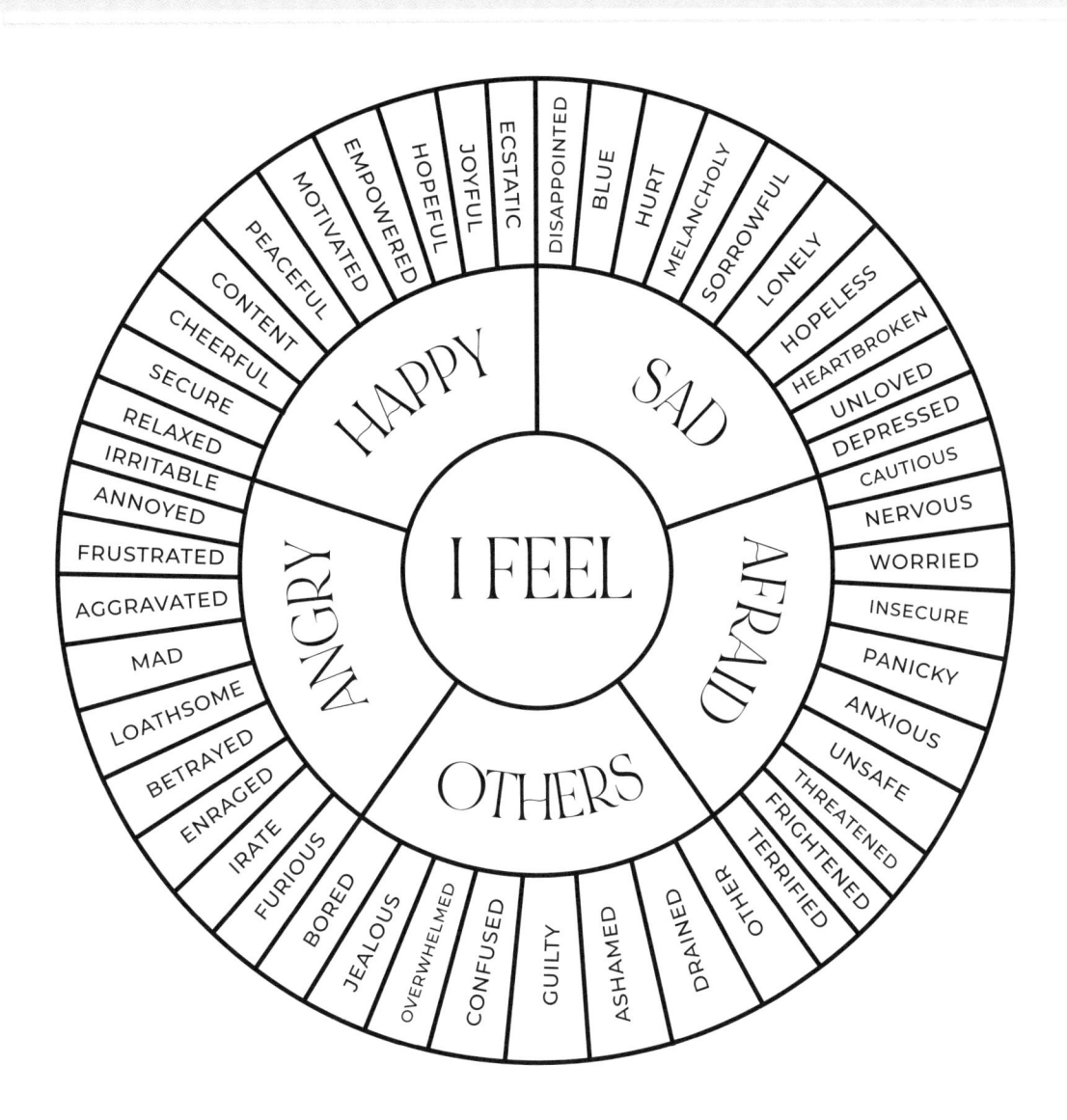

I FEEL

HAPPY: ECSTATIC, JOYFUL, HOPEFUL, EMPOWERED, MOTIVATED, PEACEFUL, CONTENT, CHEERFUL

SAD: DISAPPOINTED, BLUE, HURT, MELANCHOLY, SORROWFUL, LONELY, HOPELESS, HEARTBROKEN, UNLOVED, DEPRESSED

AFRAID: CAUTIOUS, NERVOUS, WORRIED, INSECURE, PANICKY, ANXIOUS, UNSAFE, THREATENED, FRIGHTENED, TERRIFIED

ANGRY: SECURE, RELAXED, IRRITABLE, ANNOYED, FRUSTRATED, AGGRAVATED, MAD, LOATHSOME, BETRAYED, ENRAGED, IRATE, FURIOUS

OTHERS: BORED, JEALOUS, OVERWHELMED, CONFUSED, GUILTY, ASHAMED, DRAINED, OTHER

What do you need?

Feelings are signals. They invite us to pay attention to what is happening around us and help dictate how we respond. Often, underneath our emotions are needs waiting to be met. The diagram below shows examples of this.

IF FEELINGS COULD TALK

SADNESS might be telling me i need **TO CRY**	**LONELINESS** might be telling me i need **CONNECTION**	**SHAME** might be telling me i need **SELF-COMPASSION**	**RESENTMENT** might be telling me i need **TO FORGIVE**
EMPTINESS might be telling me i need **TO DO SOMETHING CREATIVE**	**ANGER** might be telling me i need **TO CHECK-IN WITH MY BOUNDARIES**	**ANXIETY** might be telling me i need **TO BREATHE**	**STRESS** might be telling me i need **TO TAKE IT ONE STEP AT A TIME**

Illustration based on 'If Feelings Could Talk: A Free Social Emotional Learning Poster' by wholeheartedschoolcounseling.com

Based on how you are feeling right now, what do you need?

If you are feeling great, take a moment to celebrate this. If you are experiencing any difficult emotions, you might call someone on your support team or do something calming/uplifting like going for a walk. Refer to the diagram above for additional examples.

I FEEL

I NEED

IT'S A MIRACLE

RESILIENCE BUILDING BLOCK: CONTROL AND CONTRIBUTION

> "The future belongs to those who *believe* in the beauty of their dreams."
>
> Eleanor Roosevelt

In the darkest moments of my life, I was trapped in so much pain and chaos I didn't think I would make it to my 21st birthday. Even then, buried deep in my heart, I had this vision for what I wanted my life to look like. I would go on walks through a nearby neighborhood and marvel at the homes with green lawns and children's toys scattered about. I dreamed of having an intact family where we would all have the same last name. I dreamed of laughter-filled dinners around a table and impromptu dance parties with giggling children. This tucked away dream beckoned me to better days.

Visualizing and dreaming about a brighter future is an act of reclaiming our power. It is a way of asserting that our past does not define us, and that we have the ability to shape our own lives. By envisioning a future filled with joy, peace, wholeness, and contentment, we take an active role in rewriting our narrative.

When we find ourselves overwhelmed by the pain and challenges of life or devastated by loss or betrayal, fear of further disappointment can tempt us to stop dreaming. But, when we allow ourselves to dream and visualize a better future, we tap into a wellspring of hope. It becomes a beacon of light that can guide us through the healing process and inspire us to take steps towards creating the life we desire.

Maybe you are in a season where it is hard to dream. Perhaps you have closed off that part of yourself that was once wild with imagination and lofty goals. Please know that it is okay to start small. Begin by imagining moments of peace, joy and contentment. Eventually, you can allow yourself to dream without limitations or judgment. Embrace the possibilities that lie ahead and know that you deserve a future filled with love, joy, and fulfillment.

IMAGINE

Dream with me for a moment.

First, find a quiet place. Take a few, slow deep breaths.

Now, imagine you can see your future self living a thriving life- unhindered by fear or trauma or scarcity. What do you notice about your future self? What are you doing? Who are you with? Who is there? Who is not there? What do you see? What do you hear? What do you feel when you imagine this?

Now, imagine you wake up tomorrow and a miracle has happened. All of your problems are solved. Life is going the way you hoped it would. It might feel far away or even impossible, but use your heart's imagination to explore what that might look like.

Scan the QR Code to experience Harmony talking you through this visualization.

REFLECT

What would be different? What would the signs be that the miracle occurred?

Has your life ever looked like this before?
If so, what was different?

What would it take for this miracle to occur?

Looking back, has there been a time in your life when things were better than they are now? What was different?

WISDOM TO KNOW THE DIFFERENCE

RESILIENCE BUILDING BLOCKS: COMPETENCE, CONFIDENCE, COPING AND CONTROL

> "You *can't* keep the birds from flying over your head, but you *can* keep them from building a nest in your hair."
>
> — Proverbs

My mom battled with substance abuse beginning when she was 12 years-old. I understand now that she was using drugs to escape a long history of trauma that she didn't have the tools to cope with. When I was in middle school, she began attending Cocaine and Narcotics Anonymous meetings to get sober. Because she didn't have childcare, my brother and I would often tag along. It was in those meetings that I first heard the Serenity Prayer.

God, grant me the Serenity to accept the things I cannot change,
Courage to change the things I can,
and Wisdom to know the difference.

Back then, I wasn't much of a praying person, but this particular prayer stuck with me and I prayed it repeatedly. Often, I prayed it several times a day, and sometimes, I prayed it over and over, almost obsessively.

For many years, I mostly focused on the part about accepting the things I could not change. I recognized that I could not change my "boyfriend" aka pimp. I couldn't get him to be kind, to cherish me, to respect me, to stop sleeping with other women…to stop pimping other women. I felt powerless and out of control. I was too afraid to leave, so I prayed that I would learn to accept the dysfunction I could not change.

It took me a long while to finally realize that I was not as powerless and helpless as I felt. Yes, I needed to accept the things I could not change, but I also needed the courage to change the things I could.

I finally started focusing on what I could change... me.

I could change my boundaries, what I would allow or not allow, give or not give. Whether I would stay or leave.

Safety Check

If you are in an unsafe situation, we encourage you to get additional help.

Domestic Violence Hotline: 800-799-7233
National Trafficking Hotline: 888-373-7888

If you are in immediate danger, please call 911.

WHAT IS IN MY CONTROL?

Focusing on what we *cannot* control produces anxiety, worry, and helplessness. Focusing on what we *can* control fosters a sense of empowerment and security.

In order to help us determine what is in our control and what is not, sometimes it is helpful to see it on paper. Here is an example of what that might look like:

WHAT IS NOT MY CONTROL?

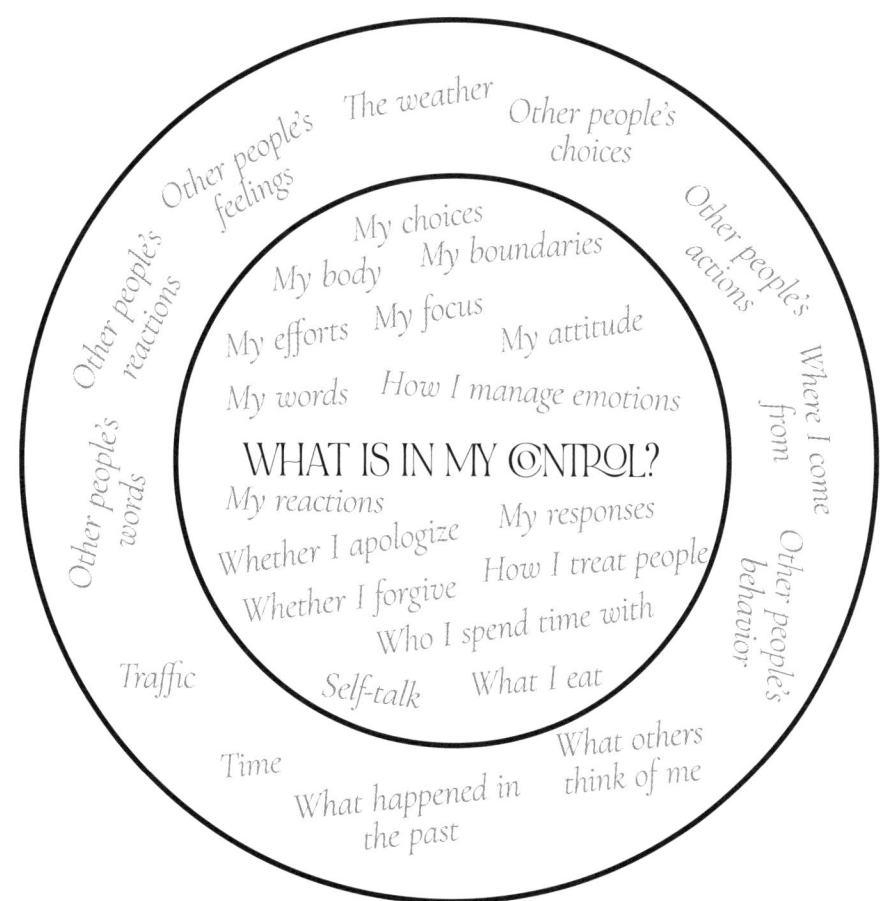

- Other people's feelings
- The weather
- Other people's choices
- Other people's actions
- Where I come from
- Other people's behavior
- Other people's words
- Other people's reactions
- Traffic
- Time
- What happened in the past
- What others think of me

WHAT IS IN MY CONTROL?

- My choices
- My body
- My boundaries
- My efforts
- My focus
- My attitude
- My words
- How I manage emotions
- My reactions
- My responses
- Whether I apologize
- How I treat people
- Whether I forgive
- Who I spend time with
- Self-talk
- What I eat

WHEN CONTROL HAS BEEN TAKEN FROM US

Even as I filled in the diagram above, I am reminded that some of us have been in relationships with people who have controlled areas of our lives that should have been in our control. In these situations, sometimes control is taken from us; other times, for various reasons, we may give away our control. For example, I know that I should be able to determine what I eat and who I spend time with. However, there was a time in my life when my exploiter controlled these aspects of my life. I should also be able to control what happens to my body, but the painful reality is, that has not always been the case.

As you reflect on the diagram above, you may notice areas of your life that have been controlled by others. Facing that fact might be understandably difficult. If you find yourself needing some support or need to process this more, I encourage you to reach out to one of the people you identified as part of your support system.

YOUR TURN

When you consider all the things that are concerning you right now, what is in your control? What is out of your control? Use the diagram below to help you sort it out.

WHAT IS NOT MY CONTROL?

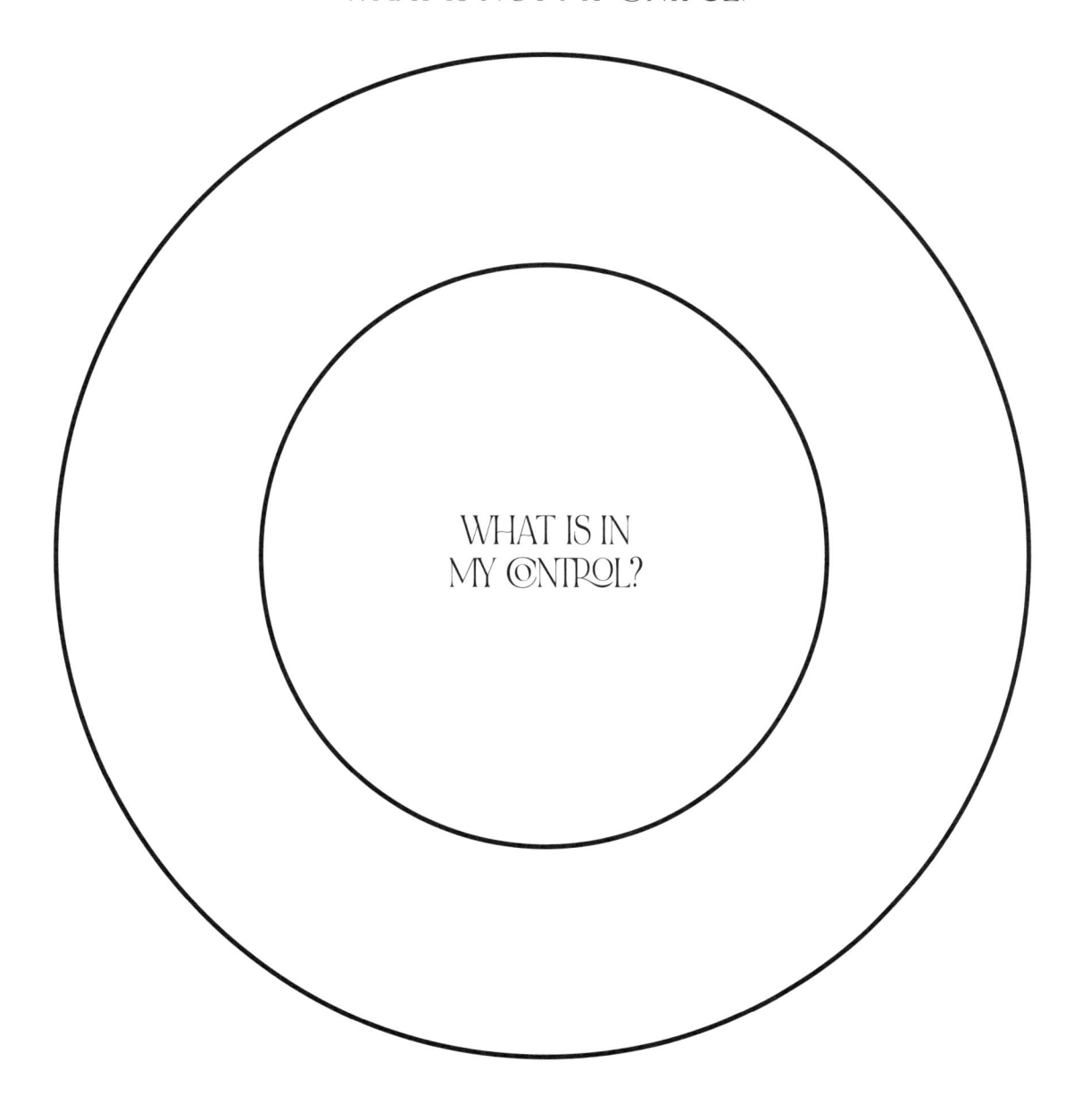

WHAT IS IN MY CONTROL?

FOCUS HERE

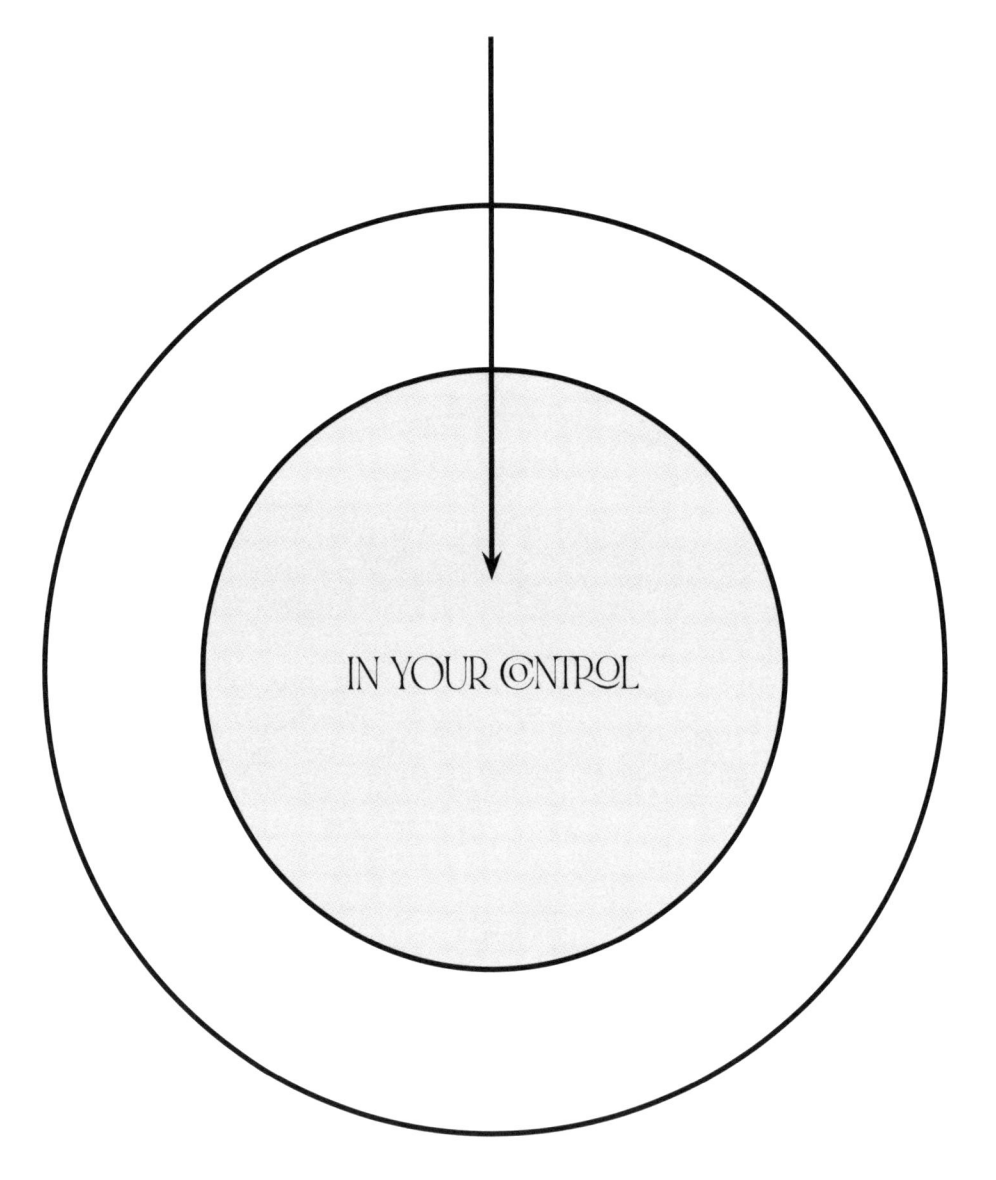

IN YOUR CONTROL

As we practice shifting our focus to the things we can control and learn to surrender those things that are outside of our control, we will begin to feel more empowered to take action that will lead to healthy change.

FREE TO CHANGE

RESILIENCE BUILDING BLOCKS: COMPETENCE AND CONTROL
AND CONTROL

> "Until the pain of staying the same is *greater* than the pain of change, most people prefer to stay the same."
>
> Dr. Richard D. Dobbins

Change is hard. No reason to sugar coat it. In my memoir, Scars and Stilettos, I shared the quote above because it is one of my favorites. I relate to it deeply. As much as I hoped to have a different life, for many, many years, change felt truly impossible. Deep inside, a sense of shame and insecurity left me believing that I didn't deserve a good life.

I was wrong.

Part of what is hard about change is it requires us to disrupt current habits and patterns while simultaneously moving toward new habits and patterns that are unfamiliar. And if there is one thing us humans don't like, it's the unfamiliar. Our instincts wire us to predict what will happen next. If "what will happen next" is uncertain, we are likely to want to stick with what is familiar.

But just because something is familiar, does not mean that it is good for us.

Leaving the sex industry was hard. It meant walking away from fast money and all of the people that I had become accustomed to. That customer I could call when I needed extra cash. The people I could call when I was lonely, even if they weren't exactly helping me live my best life. I knew that leaving meant facing financial uncertainty and a lot of loneliness. But the hardest part of all was leaving my exploiter. I didn't call him that then. I called him Derrick.

The morning of my baptism marked the beginning of what would be a new life for me. I was determined to leave all the pain – all the things I never wanted to be – right there in that water, and I was going to emerge a new person. To prepare for my fresh start, I had to cut the final tie to what was becoming my old life: Derrick. Before I made the call, all morning I had been calling credit-card companies, removing his name from accounts, canceling his cards. Once he found out I was cutting him off, I didn't want to take the chance of him going on one last shopping spree and running up my credit cards.

Finally, I picked up the phone and dialed his number. The phone rang; and rang; and rang. Please pick up! Please, please pick up! I have to do this, I thought to myself.

"Hello?" His deep voice was slow and lingering; so unsuspecting. I began to wonder if I could really go through with it.
"Hey, it's me..." I can and I will, I told myself.
"Yeah... what's up?" he said, with his usual "What do you want" kind of tone.
"I'm just calling to let you know that I can't have you in my life any more, and from now on I will no longer be supporting you financially." I spoke with more confidence than I knew I had. "It stops here. Please don't call me. Please don't try to get in touch with me."

"What? I don't understand," he stammered.

I knew the look on his face without seeing it. It was the what-the-hell-is-wrong-with-you-have-you-lost-your-mind look.

"You don't have to understand. You just have to accept it. Please don't try to call me," I replied calmly, as though I had rehearsed it a thousand times. In actuality the words just came to me. I knew that if I gave him reasons, he would have a chance to get back in my head and try to convince me I was making a mistake.

"I have to go." And with that I hung up the phone, and with it an era of my life.

Some days I had tried to imagine my life without Derrick. I had tried to picture the end of our relationship. I had always thought it would come by death – his or mine. And if he had died first, I would be sure to follow.

He was gone from me, and I was still very much alive.

Whether it means walking away from toxic people or situations, breaking free from addiction, discontinuing destructive habits, or creating new boundaries and healthier habits, to really thrive in life, we have to be willing to embrace change- or at least tolerate it.

There is a model that has helped me better understand the (often messy) process of change. We will be digging deeper into this model in future volumes of Live Free, but for now, I hope this helps you reflect on your own life and some of the changes you've been contemplating.

STAGES OF CHANGE

NOT THINKING — PRE-CONTEMPLATION

THINKING — CONTEMPLATION

PREPARATION

ACTION — MAKING CHANGES

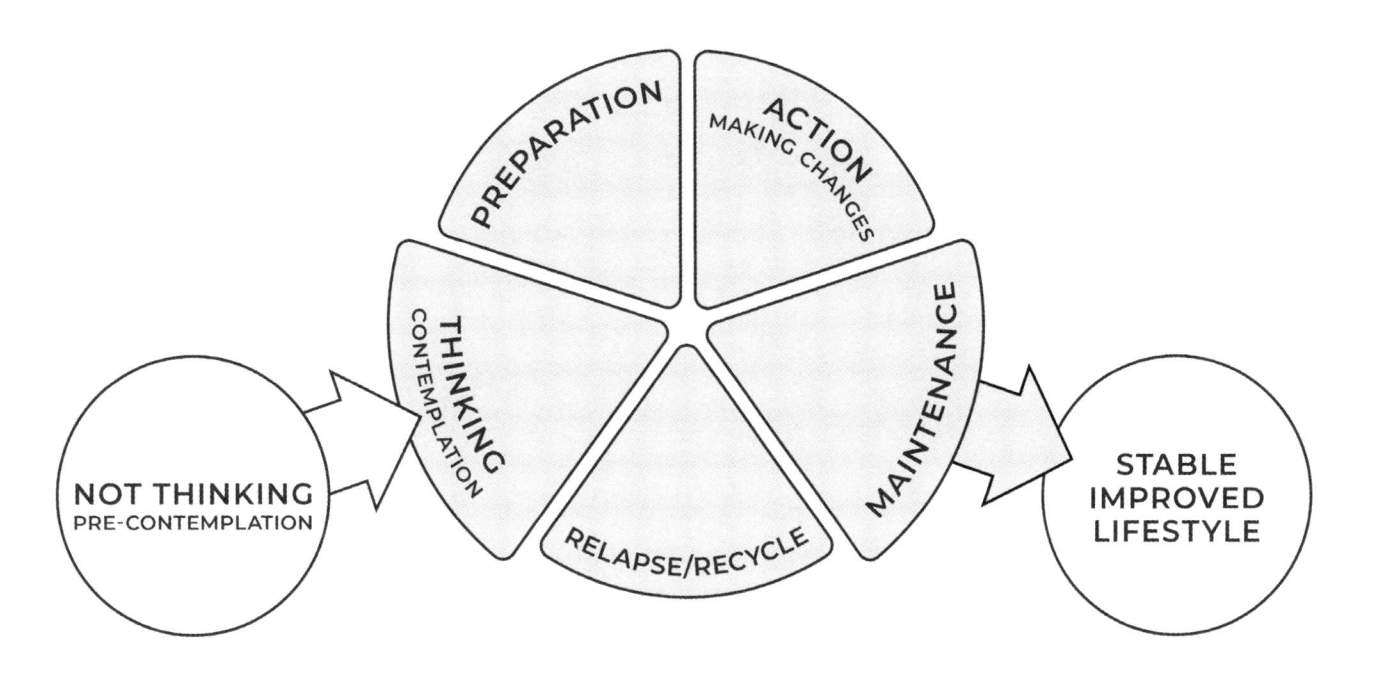

MAINTENANCE

RELAPSE/RECYCLE

STABLE IMPROVED LIFESTYLE

James Prochaska and Carlo DiClemente identified and developed their Stages of Change as one of the three components in their Transtheoretical Model of Behavior Change. I have simplified and adapted their model for this workbook.

Stage 1: Not Thinking About Change

In the first stage in the Stages of Change Model we aren't even really thinking about changing and may even be unaware of the need to change.

Stage 2: Thinking About Change

In this stage, we are thinking about change and intend to make changes in the near future. We probably still have a lot of mixed feelings about change (also known as ambivalence), which might make us want to keep putting it off.

Stage 3: Getting Ready to Change

In this stage, we are getting ready to start making changes. We begin taking small steps such as telling our friends and family that we want to change.

Stage 4: Action

In the Action stage, we have changed our behavior and need to work hard to keep moving ahead. In this stage, it is normal to think about going back to old relationships and habits. With the proper tools and support, we can keep moving forward.

Stage 5: Maintenance

We are in the Maintenance stage when we have changed our behavior more than 6 months ago. We are likely aware of the situations/people that may tempt us to slip back into unhealthy behaviors and relationships. With newfound healthy coping skills and a good support system, we will be empowered to stay the course.

Relapse/Recycling

Change is not a linear process. Often we will find ourselves returning to old habits and people. This is known as Recycling or Relapse- it is not a stage in itself, but it is the return from Action or Maintenance to an earlier stage. If and when we find ourselves in Relapse/Recycling, we can lean on our support system and use the tools we have gained to return to Action. It is important to have grace for yourself and remember that this is a normal part of the process for many people.

REFLECT

As you contemplate the stages listed above, which stage do you think you are in? (If you have already made those changes, jump to the next section, "I Already Made the Change")

What do you think you need in order to move forward in your own process?

If you were to begin to/continue to move towards healthy change in your life, what do you believe your next step would be?

You can't change what happened yesterday, *but you can decide where you will go from here.* No matter where you are, right here and now, you have what it takes to make your next step toward the healthy life you deserve.

MIXED FEELINGS ABOUT CHANGE

Having mixed feelings about change just means we are human. In my own journey, one minute I would decide I was completely fed up and ready to leave the industry and the relationship that was keeping me there and the next, I was second-guessing myself.

I would find myself overwhelmed thinking about the bills I had and the back-up plan I didn't have yet. "Maybe next month," I would tell myself.

These mixed feelings about change are called ambivalence. They are completely normal. They are also important to explore.

One of the things that is helpful in processing these feelings is to create a Pros and Cons list. This will help you get more clarity on what is really at stake in your life.

If you find yourself overwhelmed by all of the changes you want to make, I want to remind you that this is a process. Please approach this with self-compassion and grace, knowing that all you have to do is take one step at a time. I encourage you to focus on exploring the ONE change that feels most meaningful to you right now.

NOTE: If you have already made the changes you wanted to make, you may skip to the section below titled, "I Already Made the Change."

REFLECT

Name that change... what change are you exploring?

	PROS	CONS
CHANGING		
NOT CHANGING		

WHAT DO YOU NEED?

If you were to take steps towards the change you are exploring, what do you think you would need to succeed? Examples may include seeking support from a mentor, sponsor, therapist, or ally; learning healthy coping strategies; making a change in your environment; or setting a new boundary.

I ALREADY MADE THE CHANGE

If you have already made the changes you wanted to make or left the situation/relationship you wanted to leave, now is a great time to remind yourself why. When things get hard or you are tempted to go back, you can remind yourself of these things… Write down the following:

> Why I left/made the change. (Pros)

> What would it cost if I went back? What would I lose?

THE NEXT BEST STEP

I hope that this has been helpful and encouraging to you. If you find yourself feeling overwhelmed right now, I want to remind you of this:

"The journey of a thousand miles begins with a single step."
~Lao Tzu

You don't have to have everything figured out. No need to get all caught up worrying about the steps you might take tomorrow. If you take it one day at a time, one moment at a time, one step at a time, you can make the entire journey that way.
I encourage you to sit with this question:

"What is one thing I can do today that will be a step towards the future I want?"

Because you are worth it!

My next best step is....

Safety Check

If you are in an unsafe situation, we encourage you to get additional help.

Domestic Violence Hotline: 800-799-7233
National Trafficking Hotline: 888-373-7888

If you are in immediate danger, please call 911.

A LEAP OF FAITH

RESILIENCE BUILDING BLOCKS: CONNECTION, COMPETENCE AND CONTROL

> "Sometimes your only available transportation is *a leap of faith.*"
>
> — Margaret Shepard

As I contemplated leaving the life I had become accustomed to, I was left with a lot of unknowns:

How will I pay my bills?
Who will hire me?
If I try to build a new life, what will happen if people find out about my past?
How will I cope if I give up maladaptive coping mechanisms?
How will I bear the loneliness if I end that relationship?
Will anyone ever love me?
Can I truly learn to love myself?

When I left "the life" and my exploiter, I did not have answers to these questions.

Moving towards a thriving life requires courage. It often means that we will need to take a leap into the discomfort of uncertainty. Embracing positive change will require taking risks, trusting the process and being open to new possibilities.

For some, a leap of faith will feel supported and sustained by a faith in God. My personal path towards a thriving life has been deeply connected to my faith journey. Inviting God into my process was the catalyst for every other leap of faith I have taken. Discovering that I have been created with a purpose and I don't have to be perfect to be perfectly loved has been a game-changer for me. Believing in a God who is kind, generous and forgiving—a God who fights for me and believes in me— has given me the strength and courage I needed to fight for myself.

Maybe what I am describing isn't resonating with you. Maybe you have experienced religious wounds. Or perhaps you don't identify as a person of faith at all. I am not here to judge, fix, or change you. I am in no place to do so. I want you to know that I acknowledge and honor your experiences and beliefs.

But if what I am sharing is resonating with you, the upcoming exercise, "Imagine" will give you an opportunity to connect more deeply with God. I, personally, have found this activity to be very meaningful.

At the end of the day, faith is about having trust or confidence in something.

One of my favorite definitions of faith is this:

Faith is the confidence in what we hope for, the assurance of things unseen. ~Hebrews 11:1

Whatever we believe requires faith.

It takes faith to believe that you will fail.
It takes faith to believe that you will succeed.

Often, it takes a leap of faith to live a thriving life.

If you find yourself wanting to take a leap of faith but are feeling held back by fear, insecurity, or even pressure from those around you to stay where you are, as you are, I want to encourage you to bravely push through.

Maybe today is the day you release your fears, choose confidence, and let that voice inside of you, telling you to take that leap, ring louder than the voices of any haters or naysayers.

REFLECT

> Do you sense an invitation to take a leap of faith? If so, what does that look like?

IMAGINE

For those who are interested in including spiritual faith into their process, I am including this exercise because I believe it is a powerful one. Feel free to invite the presence of Love into this safe space of your imagination if that feels more accessible to you at this time.

Find a quiet place. Take a few, slow deep breaths.

Now, imagine yourself somewhere safe. Maybe it is somewhere you have been before, maybe it is somewhere you have dreamed of going. What do you see? What do you smell? What do you hear?

As you continue to imagine yourself in this safe place, where is God (The presence of Love)? Does He feel close? Far away? What would it look like to invite Him closer?

Still using your heart's imagination, what would it look like to give your cares and concerns to Him? Would you lay them at His feet? Would you allow Him to lift the heavy weight from
your back?

Once you have done this, is there something He wants to give you in exchange? Is it His peace? Joy? Healing? Forgiveness? Something else? What does it look like? Smell like? Feel like?

**Scan the QR Code to experience Harmony
talking you through this visualization.**

REFLECT

After you have finished the exercise above, write down what you saw, felt and experienced.

If you found this practice to be helpful, you can revisit it anytime. Repeat it as often as you would like to reground yourself in the beauty and goodness that is available to you.

Check Your Feelings

Now that you have completed a few more sections, it's time for another feelings check-in...

TOO MUCH TOO SOON?

If naming your feelings is too much too soon, you can circle one of the thumbs below that best describes your mood and move onto the next section.

👍 ✋ 👎

Ready to name your feelings?

Using the chart below, circle which feeling(s) you are having...

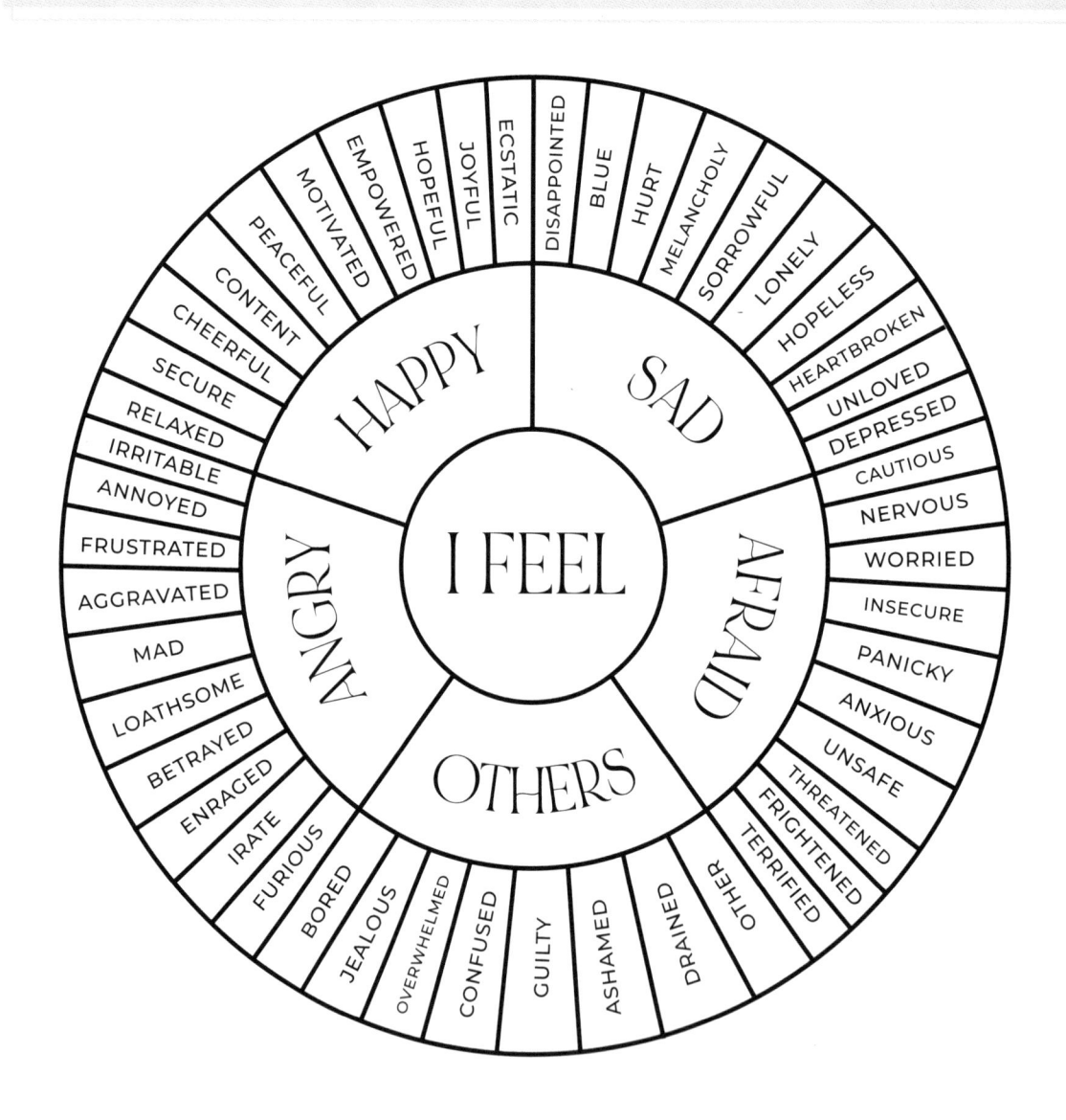

I FEEL

HAPPY: ECSTATIC, JOYFUL, HOPEFUL, EMPOWERED, MOTIVATED, PEACEFUL, CONTENT, CHEERFUL, SECURE, RELAXED

SAD: DISAPPOINTED, BLUE, HURT, MELANCHOLY, SORROWFUL, LONELY, HOPELESS, HEARTBROKEN, UNLOVED, DEPRESSED

AFRAID: CAUTIOUS, NERVOUS, WORRIED, INSECURE, PANICKY, ANXIOUS, UNSAFE, THREATENED, FRIGHTENED, TERRIFIED

ANGRY: IRRITABLE, ANNOYED, FRUSTRATED, AGGRAVATED, MAD, LOATHSOME, BETRAYED, ENRAGED, IRATE, FURIOUS

OTHERS: BORED, JEALOUS, OVERWHELMED, CONFUSED, GUILTY, ASHAMED, DRAINED, OTHER

What do you need?

Feelings are signals. They invite us to pay attention to what is happening around us and help dictate how we respond. Often, underneath our emotions are needs waiting to be met. The diagram below shows examples of this.

IF FEELINGS COULD TALK

SADNESS might be telling me i need **TO CRY**	**LONELINESS** might be telling me i need **CONNECTION**	**SHAME** might be telling me i need **SELF-COMPASSION**	**RESENTMENT** might be telling me i need **TO FORGIVE**
EMPTINESS might be telling me i need **TO DO SOMETHING CREATIVE**	**ANGER** might be telling me i need **TO CHECK-IN WITH MY BOUNDARIES**	**ANXIETY** might be telling me i need **TO BREATHE**	**STRESS** might be telling me i need **TO TAKE IT ONE STEP AT A TIME**

Illustration based on 'If Feelings Could Talk: A Free Social Emotional Learning Poster' by wholeheartedschoolcounseling.com

Based on how you are feeling right now, what do you need?

If you are feeling great, take a moment to celebrate this. If you are experiencing any difficult emotions, you might call someone on your support team or do something calming/uplifting like going for a walk. Refer to the diagram above for additional examples.

I FEEL

I NEED

YOU DID IT!

> *"You are still here.* You have made it to the end of this volume, and you have made it through so much more."

I hope you are proud of yourself.

Completing this workbook is a significant step towards the beautiful, thriving life you were meant to live.

Through this process, you have shown resilience and an unwavering commitment to your own healing. I hope that reflecting on how far you have come will fuel you to continue to show up for yourself, day after day.

Because you are worth it!

As you move forward, I want to encourage you to
make 2 commitments to yourself:

1. Embrace self-compassion. Be gentle and kind to yourself as you continue on your journey. It's natural to have moments of doubt or setbacks. Remember that this process is not linear, and it's okay to have ups and downs. Offer yourself compassion, understanding, and forgiveness. We owe it to ourselves to do the best we can, and we can breathe a sigh of relief knowing "the best we can" is enough.

☐   I commit to embracing self-compassion.

_____

SIGN HERE

2. Develop and lean on your support system. Safe people who respect your boundaries and cheer you on as you move towards your most thriving life are absolutely vital. Remember, building relationships takes time and effort. Be patient with yourself and allow connections to develop, naturally. Seek out individuals who have demonstrated empathy, respect, and a commitment to supporting your healing process. Surround yourself with those who uplift and inspire you.

While life may have its ups and downs, having safe people by your side can provide stability, strength, and encouragement.

☐ I commit to developing and leaning on my support system.

_____

SIGN HERE

Remember...your past does not determine your future.

The obstacles you are facing are no match for the incredible potential that lies within you. You have what it takes to reach the thriving life you have dreamed of.

One step at a time.

You've got this! I believe in you!

Love,

Harmony

KEEP THRIVING

The next volumes of the Live Free Series and other resources to help you on your journey are available in our store.

ABOUT THE AUTHOR

Harmony Dust, MSW

I am best known for overcoming a history of abuse and exploitation, a story I share in my memoir, Scars and Stilettos, and for founding Treasures (2003), a survivor-led outreach and support group to women in the sex industry and survivors of sex trafficking.

I am thankful for the opportunity to use my pain for purpose.

AND...I am more than a survivor of sexual exploitation.
I am a lover of God, salsa dancing, hammocks, and the towering beauty of mature oak trees. I play a mean game of spades, dominoes, and popeye.

I love standing at the edge of the ocean and watching the way the sun sparkles on the waves. I love long, lingering dinners set to the sound of jazz, laughter and meaningful conversation. I love dancing until I am out of breath and have forgotten all of my worries.

I am also a Mama. My spunky, creative daughter keeps me on my toes and my kind-hearted son brings joy to everyone he meets.

ABOUT TREASURES

Founded in 2003, Treasures is a survivor-led organization whose mission is to equip and empower women in the sex industry and survivors of trafficking to live healthy, flourishing lives and train others to do the same across the globe. For more information, please visit **www.iamatreasure.com**

MORE RESOURCES

Available at: **www.iamatreasure.com**

SCARS AND STILETTOS

At thirteen, after being abandoned by her mother one summer and left to take care of her younger brother, Harmony becomes susceptible to a relationship that turns out to be toxic, abusive, and ultimately exploitative. She eventually finds herself working in a strip club at the age of nineteen, and her boyfriend becomes her pimp, controlling her every move and taking all of her money. Ultimately, she discovers a path to freedom and a whole new life.

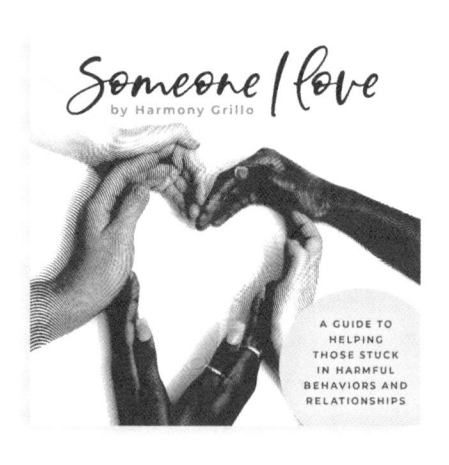

SOMEONE I LOVE

In this short, interactive guide, you'll learn how to support your loved one when they are engaged in harmful patterns, behaviors, and relationships. No matter how deep in despair your loved one may be, there is hope. And you have an opportunity to play a vital role in their journey to freedom. This interactive guide will show you how!

TREASURES ONLINE TRAINING

Want to help women in the sex industry and survivors of trafficking find lasting freedom and healing? Treasures Training is for you if you want to...

- Effectively support women in the sex industry and survivors of trafficking
- Better understand trauma and exploitation
- Start a strip-club ministry or outreach

YOU CAN MAKE AN IMPACT.
WE'LL SHOW YOU HOW.

Since 2007, we have trained hundreds of leaders, including members of the FBI, DOJ, social workers, law enforcement, churches and NGOs worldwide. Now in digital form, our training is more accessible than ever to you and your volunteer team.

Included in the training
- 6+ hours of video training
- Treasures Training manual
- Quiz questions to ensure understanding
- Sample documents
- Support Group Guidelines
- Outreach Training (Only Outreach and Care Track)
- Volunteer Training (Only Outreach and Care Track)
- "Should Prostitution be Legal" Bonus Video
- "Sex Sells" Bonus Video

To learn more or enroll, visit:
https://www.iamatreasure.com/trainingso

"Whenever you find yourself doubting how far you can go, just remember how far you have come. Remember everything you have faced, all the battles you have won and all the fears you have overcome."
-Unknown

Notes

Notes

Notes